Blue Geopolitics

Transnational Institute Series

The Transnational Institute is an independent fellowship of researchers and activists living in different parts of the world, who develop innovative analyses of world affairs.

It serves no government, political party or interest group.

Blue Geopolitics

The United Nations Reform and the Future of the Blue Helmets

Vicenç Fisas

Translated by Andrew Langdon Davies
Foreword by Federico Mayor Zaragoza,
Director General of UNESCO

Pluto Press

LONDON • EAST HAVEN, CT

with

Transnational Institute (TNI)

First published in Spanish by ICARIA 1994

First English edition published 1995
by Pluto Press, 345 Archway Road,
London N6 5AA
and 140 Commerce Street,
East Haven, CT 06512, USA
in association with
the Transnational Institute (TNI),
Paulus Potterstraat 20, 1071 DA, Amsterdam

British Library Cataloguing in Publication Data
A catalogue record for this book is available from the British Library

ISBN 0 7453 1032 X

Library of Congress Cataloging-in-Publication Data
Fisas Armangol, Vicenç
  [Desafío de Naciones Unidas ante el mundo en crisis. English]
  Blue geopolitics: the United Nations reform and the future of the
  blue helmets/Vicenç Fisas: translated by Andrew Langdon Davies:
  foreword by Frederico Mayor Zaragoza. — 1st English ed.
    p.   cm. — (Transnational Institute series)
  Includes index.
  ISBN 0–7453–1032–X (hb)
    1. United Nations—Armed Forces. 2. United Nations—
  Reorganization. I. Title. II. Series.
  JX1981.P7F52   1995
  341.5—dc20   95–20258
                                                                     CIP

Designed and produced for Pluto Press by
Chase Production Services, Chipping Norton, OX7 5QR
Typeset from disk by Stanford Desktop Publishing Services
Printed in the EC by T J Press, Padstow, England

Contents

Figures

Tables

About the Author

Vicenç Fisas (born Barcelona, 1952) is a disarmament researcher at the UNESCO Centre of Catalonia. He has a PhD in Peace Studies from the University of Bradford (UK) and is a defence researcher for the Peace Research Centre in Madrid, a member of the Saragossa Peace Research Seminar and a political analyst for Médecins Sans Frontières. He is the author of twenty books on peace, disarmament and conflict. He was awarded the National Prize for Human Rights in 1988.

The author wishes to thank the considerable and valuable documentary help provided by Mariano Aguirre (CIP), of the UN Information Office in Spain and the Spanish delegation of the UNHCR in preparing the original manuscript for the Catalan edition of this book, published by UNESCO Centre of Catalonia, and for updating the English edition. The Spanish edition was made possible thanks to the help of the Saragossa Peace Research Seminar.

Foreword

The pace of events is dizzying. Our communications technologies present images of the world around us which are rapidly replaced by new information which is equally short-lived. Current affairs cloud our vision of the enormous changes that are profoundly affecting humanity today. Serene reflection on events will reveal to us the great transformations affecting us.

First of all, we see a widespread move towards common values acceptable to all human beings and all human societies. This search is a result of the new awareness on common problems affecting the whole of humanity. We are concerned about the inordinate growth of the world's population, in view of the fact that the planet's resources are limited and that we cannot grow indefinitely. We are concerned about a system of economic relations that leads to shocking differences between countries and within each society. We are concerned about a development model, a technological structure, that shows no respect for the environment or for future genera-tions. These challenges call for agreement on global ethics which will allow us to direct our knowledge and our energies in the right direction. Local or group interests must be fitted into a new sense of global responsibility. Religions, cultures and governmental and non-governmental organisations must all contribute to the creation of a new spirit of universal solidarity. Peace must be encouraged in the conviction that we are all members of the same human family.

Secondly, we see a growing interest in human diversity. It is true there is still racism and intolerance, but we are progressing towards a society that respects differences. People are gradually realising that cultural, linguistic, religious, ethnical, ideological and national diversity are all part of the wealth of life. Governing societies does not mean reducing diversity, so much as organising it harmoniously. Wars have often come about through one group's wish to dominate another. At present we are moving towards recognition of the fact that all cultures are equal in dignity, that individuals with roots in one culture are enriched when they take an interest in other cultures, and that political structures are needed that allow all cultures to develop and grow. All societies today are multicultural. This does not mean that our cultural future has to be characterised by a lack of roots or that there will only be room for certain demographically more powerful languages and cultures. We aspire to a future in which small cultures are respected and can contribute to universality through particularity. The recognition of diversity is one of the bases for the democracy of the future. Democracy also means recognising the rights of all cultural groups, including their right to self-government. Love of diversity is one of the roads to peace.

Thirdly, we see a tendency to relativise state structures which for centuries have been the usual way of organising power. Today, part of the sovereignty of states is being transferred to regional or global international organisations while, within states, power is also being transferred to more reduced territories to make democracy more participative. The political maps of all the continents will in future evolve and outgrow the outdated nature of borders and permit new political structures corresponding more closely to human realities and popular aspirations. In recent years the international community has accepted that there are limits to the old principle of non-interference in the internal affairs of each state. The priorities are respect for human rights, humanitarian aid and, in general, to intervene in actions that could affect international peace and security. The present concept of security is very different to the one generally accepted just a few years ago. Before it seemed that military security – in other words, armament – was the key element in security. Now we know that new approaches must be found and that what is needed is, paradoxically, progressive and general disarmament. In this respect, the tradition of state armies belongs to the past rather than to the future. Peace will be possible if the political order represented by the state evolves towards a new, more rational, political order.

The United Nations Organisation is at present the political structure that best represents the great ideological and political transformations of humanity. Its still modest reality corresponds very closely to the developments I speak of. The Organisation provides room for a universal dialogue, through which it has been possible to agree on certain values shared by all cultures and traditions. The Organisation has established practices of democratic political collaboration on the principle of the recognition of diversity, and it hopes to create universal political structures able to surpass the limitations of state powers.

We must accept that the Organisation is still at an early stage. For many years the division of the world into two antagonistic political blocs paralysed the Organisation's possibilities. Since 1989 a new period has got under way, but there are a lot of obstacles to be overcome. The United Nations Member States, especially the most powerful, find it difficult to accept a moral and political power higher than their own. At the moment there is still a strong temptation to make the Organisation serve interests that are hardly universal. Non-governmental organisations (NGOs) are generally more sensitive to universal interests. The contradictions of many Member States are all too evident. I think that only a change of mentality among politicians, scientists, the military, journalists, teachers, technicians and cultural agents of all sorts can guarantee a renewed United Nations capable of answering the great challenges of our age. We at UNESCO are working with the objective of creating a new culture of peace. We want to be the conscience and the driving force for this new way of thinking and acting. This book by Vicenç Fisas, a researcher at the UNESCO Centre of Catalonia, is an outstanding contribution to the reflections arising all over the world on the present and future of the United Nations, precisely in 1995, the year we celebrate the 50th anniversary of the Organisation. Vicenç Fisas's research centres on the United Nations Peace-keeping Forces, but it provides a series of more general analyses on security issues and on the structures desirable for the Organisation. I hope it will contribute to a serious debate on the necessary reorientation of our political future and on the future of that fragile but marvellous instrument, the United Nations Organisation. By doing so, *Blue Geopolitics* will reduce the distance between Utopia and reality.

Federico Mayor Zaragoza
Director General of UNESCO

Acronyms

ACDA	US Arms Control and Disarmament Agency
APAR	International Convention on the Suppression and Punishment of the Crime of Apartheid (1973)
AWACS	Airborne Warning and Control System
BW	Biological Weapons
C3I	Command, Control, Communications and Intelligence
C4I	Command, Control, Communications, Co-operation and Intelligence
CAMDUN-2	Second Conference for a More Democratic United Nations
CAT	Convention against Torture and Other Cruel, Inhuman or Degrading forms of Treatment or Punishment (1984)
CBM	Confidence-building Measures
CCPR	International Covenant on Civil and Political Rights (1966)
CEDAW	Convention on the Elimination of All Forms of Discrimination against Women (1979)
CERD	International Convention on the Elimination of All Forms of Racial Discrimination (1989)
CESCR	International Covenant on Economic, Social and Cultural Rights (1986)
CFE-1A	Treaty of Conventional Armed Forces in Europe (Act of the Negotiation on Personnel Strength)
CIS	Commonwealth of Independent States
CPC	Conflict Prevention Centre
CRC	Convention on the Rights of the Child (1986)
CSC	Commissions for Security and Confidence Creation
CSCE	Conference on Security and Co-operation in Europe
CSO	Committee of Senior Officials
ECOWAS	Economic Organisation of West African States
ECMO	European Collective Military Organisation
ECSO	European Collective Security Organisation

FAO	Food and Agriculture Organisation of the United Nations
FOB	Forward Operative Base
GIEWS	Global Information and Early Warning System
GIWS	Global Information and Warning System for Food and Agriculture
GNP	Gross National Product
HCNM	High Commissioner for National Minorities
IAEA	International Atomic Energy Agency
ICJ	International Court of Justice
IMF	International Monetary Fund
IOM	International Organisation for Migration
MINURSO	United Nations Mission for the Referendum in Western Sahara
MSF	Médecins Sans Frontières
NACC	North Atlantic Co-operation Council
NATO	North Atlantic Treaty Organisation
NGO	Non-governmental Organisations
OAS	Organisation of American States
OAU	Organisation of African Unity
OECD	Organisation for Economic Co-operation and Development
ONUC	United Nations Operation in the Congo
ONUCA	United Nations Observer Group in Central America
ONUMOZ	United Nations Operation in Mozambique
ONUSAL	United Nations Observer Mission in El Salvador
ONUSOM	United Nations Operation in Somalia
OPI	Optional Protocol to the International Covenant on Civil and Political Rights (1966)
OPI2	Second Optional Protocol to the International Covenant on Civil and Political Rights Aimed at the Abolition of Capital Punishment (1989)
ORCI	Office of Research and Collection of Information
OSCE	Organisation on Security and Cooperation in Europe (formerly CSCE)
PEF	Peace Enforcement Force
PKF	Peace-keeping Force
PKO	Peace-keeping Operation
PSU	Peace Safeguarding Unit
SG	Secretary General
SIPRI	Stockholm International Peace Research Institute
UN	United Nations
UNAMIR	United Nations Assistance Mission for Rwanda

UNASOG	United Nations Aouzov Strip Observer Group
UNAVEM	United Nations Angola Verification Mission
UNAVEM II	United Nations Angola Verification Mission II
UNDOF	United Nations Disengagement Observer Force
UNDP	United Nations Development Programme
UNEF I	First United Nations Emergency Force
UNEF II	Second United Nations Emergency Force
UNESCO	United Nations Educational, Scientific and Cultural Organisation
UNFICYP	United Nations Peace-keeping Force in Cyprus
UNGOMAP	United Nations Good Offices Mission in Afghanistan and Pakistan
UNHCR	United Nations High Commissioner for Refugees
UNICEF	United Nations Children's Fund
UNIFIL	United Nations Interim Force in Lebanon
UNIIMOG	United Nations Iran–Iraq Military Observer Group
UNIKOM	United Nations Iraq–Kuwait Observation Mission
UNMIH	United Nations Mission in Haiti
UNMOGIP	United Nations Military Observer Group in India and Pakistan
UNOMIG	United Nations Observer Mission in Georgia
UNOMIL	United Nations Observer Mission in Liberia
UNOMSA	United Nations Observer Mission in South Africa
UNOMUR	United Nations Observer Mission Uganda–Rwanda
UNOSOM	United Nations Operation in Somalia
UNPROFOR	United Nations Protection Force
UNTAC	United Nations Transitional Authority in Cambodia
UNTAG	United Nations Transition Assistance Group
UNTSO	United Nations Truce Supervision Organisation
UNVA	United Nations Verification Agency
WEU	West European Union
WFP	World Food Programme

1

The United Nations' Overdue Reform

1995 is the 50th anniversary of the founding of the United Nations. During this time the world has undergone a profound transformation: new countries have emerged, global population has doubled, the production of petrol and cars has been multiplied by six, technology has developed to a point almost unthinkable half a century ago, human beings have walked on the moon, television has shown its great power to shape behaviour, and progress in the world of telecommunications means that we now have almost instantaneous information on any event taking place on our planet. Whether for better, in some areas, or for worse, in other fields, the world today is undoubtedly quite different from what it was in 1945.

When the United Nations Charter was signed, on 26 June 1945, the introduction stated that the signee governments were determined to preserve future generations from the scourge of war, to reaffirm faith in human rights and in the dignity and value of individuals, to promote social progress and raise the standard of living, to show tolerance and ensure that armed force is not used except for the service of the common good.

The overall results of this half century do not invite optimism as regards a large number of these commitments. War has spread, conflicts are still 'dealt with' by means of threats and coercion, the gap between rich and poor countries has widened, tolerance is still thin on the ground, and no government seems to be prepared to give up the use of armed force.

In this historical context, the organisation responsible for 'maintaining peace and international security, developing friendly relations between nations based on the principle of equal rights, achieving international co-operation in solving international problems, and being a centre for harmonising the actions of nations in the attainment of these common ends' (from Article 1 of the Charter) can hardly be said to have carried out its functions successfully. It is probably true that if the United Nations had not existed things would have been worse; but there is no doubt that the United Nations by itself has not been enough and has proved incapable of halting or detaining

1

a number of destructive processes. However, it would be unfair to forget that the United Nations does not act independently, is not a completely autonomous body, but a forum for the desires, wishes, uncertainties and power games of its Member States' foreign policies.[1]

Nevertheless, and in spite of these limitations and this unimpressive record, today's world has greater need than ever of an organisation of this nature, but one more closely in touch with the present and free of the historical bonds that led to its formation in 1945. Our point of reference today is not and cannot be the Second World War. The first challenge therefore is to determine the new world context justifying the existence of the United Nations. And if it makes sense for an organisation like the United Nations to exist, then it must be made efficient and operative, must satisfy the demands of the present moment and prepare for the future with more success than it has had during the first 50 years of life.

The United Nations Secretary General, Boutros Boutros-Ghali, has indicated the year 1995 as the deadline for a partial renovation of the organisation. The in-depth reform will take longer. The objective: to make it work properly, with legitimacy and authority. The problem is how to bring about this transformation and overdue reform.

Defining the Frame of Action

In his *Agenda for Peace*,[2] in July 1992, Boutros Boutros-Ghali laid down the five basic objectives that the work of the United Nations ought to pursue:

- Preventive diplomacy (eliminating sources of danger).
- Peace-making (solving the problems of the conflict).
- Peace-keeping (preserving peace).
- Peace-building (national reconstruction).
- Putting an end to the underlying causes of conflicts, especially economic desperation, social injustices and political oppression.

Boutros Boutros-Ghali's proposal is based on the concept of 'positive peace', which defines peace as the absence or end of all forms of violence, rather than just the absence of war. The subject of his analysis is conflict, not war, and its central pillar is conflict prevention, as opposed to crisis diplomacy. This means developing early warning functions (surveillance) and the analysis of world trends (anticipation). In the last instance, the effectiveness of an organisation such as the United Nations will depend largely on its ability to detect the onset of violent situations and intervene quickly, efficiently and surely in these initial moments.

This does not rule out United Nations support for the transformation of deficient national structures and systems (something new in the proposals of a Secretary General) and for the strengthening of new democratic structures, via a sustained effort to solve basic economic, social, cultural and humanitarian problems in situations characterised by long-term conflicts.

For the United Nations Secretary General, post-conflict peace-building:

> must be linked to the comprehensive development efforts of the United Nations, political, economic, social and cultural. The objective of peace-building is to involve hostile parties in mutually beneficial undertakings which not only contribute to economic and social development but also reinforce the confidence necessary for the creation of lasting peace. Peace-building begins with practical measures to restore the civil society, reinvigorate its economy, repair the land and restore its productivity, repatriate and resettle displaced people and refugees; it also entails reducing the level of arms in society, as a component of the volatility that induces violence.[3]

Increasing demands on the United Nations Peace-keeping Forces (the blue helmets) and their presence in many conflict and post-conflict scenarios have also stirred up discussion on the United Nations' possible dissuasive or deterrent role. Although the process is still at the discussion stage and specific criteria must be clearly established to justify any international intervention and ensure that it is not selective or discriminatory, it seems clear that so-called humanitarian diplomacy, whether for purposes of aid or intervention, will be of increasing importance in the future.

Boutros Boutros-Ghali is also in favour of acting directly on the constituent elements of contemporary conflicts. Hence his insistence on special consideration for the rights of minorities, be they ethnic, religious, social or linguistic, and preventing violations of human rights before they take place. The work of the United Nations would be meaningless if it ignored the fact that most conflicts are internal, taking place within states, something which calls for greater attention and commitment to social and economic inequalities. In 1993 there was not one single interstate conflict. All 47 active armed conflicts were internal.[4] Underdevelopment, overpopulation, emigration, environmental problems and certain forms of nationalism are a source of insecurity and conflict, and cannot be solved by traditional military means. Therefore, if this new security policy really aims to get to the roots of conflict, it will have to be demilitarised and apply the most appropriate economical, political or cultural means.

The way in which conflicts are dealt with today must not put the future at stake either. Conflict prevention and regulation, like development and politics itself, must be sustainable if it is to satisfy the needs of the present without endangering those of future generations.

All these policies, from prevention to dissuasion, must be complementary and make up a homogeneous and coherent packet. The right combination of these measures in an integrated strategy is what will make it possible to build a real system of international security. What we have is a circle which starts with information, and continues with prevention and mediation, peaceful settlement of disputes, dissuasive capacity and the means to stabilise a situation conflict.

Today's world is affected by a series of global problems which need to be dealt with and solved through global mechanisms. States have fewer and fewer chances of solving these problems alone; they need the active collaboration of other countries and the participation of NGOs, business and social movements to change certain trends which hold out little hope for the future. The characteristics of the United Nations make it the most suitable organisation for detecting and analysing these problems and finding solutions.

An account of these global problems (from underdevelopment to environmental degradation, and including foreign debt, refugees, rearmament and militarisation, AIDS, drug trafficking, etc.) will give us an idea of the wide range of subjects that have to be dealt with by an organisation such as the United Nations. This is, in fact, the scope of its concerns today; what is lacking are the means and the wish to put into practice what is analysed and decided there.

Being urgent universal problems, ecological issues and sustainable development ought to be among the new priorities in the work of the United Nations and its agencies. In this respect, the Secretary General gave a timely warning in the 1992 Report when he pointed out that in recent years less than a tenth of the Official Aid to Development has been spent on programmes in critical areas of human development, such as basic education, primary health treatment, the provision of drinking water, family planning and food. And he is right to warn of the incorrect use of development aid, since international co-operation in this field is fundamental in planning survival, satisfying the basic needs of hundreds of millions of human beings and fulfilling the chief objectives set by the organisations of the United

Nations system for the year 2000, such as ensuring basic education for all children, reducing the present rate of child mortality to one third and eliminating famine.

In order to increase the decision-making capacity of the United Nations, Member States should understand that as well as stepping up and improving co-operation between the greatest possible number of states it might also be necessary to transfer certain areas of their sovereignty to the United Nations and to other regional organisations and commit themselves to freely accepted rules of conduct. This is one of the great challenges facing the reform of the United Nations, but also a necessary condition for responsibly dealing with the issues that states cannot solve for themselves. I support the recommendation in the Stockholm Initiative[5] that compliance with international rules calls for a system that more clearly defines the rights and duties of nations and that once these rights and duties have been accepted, they must be respected. These rules must, however, gradually be raised to the category of law. Or, to put it another way, the world needs a penalisation system to deal with these situations, should a country decide to act outside the system it had previously accepted.

Nevertheless, the United Nations must never be – and probably never could be – an organisation with the power to resolve every possible type of conflict. Its purpose is to look at problems, analyse them and lead them towards positive solutions, but not to solve them directly, at least most of the time. We mustn't forget that the United Nations system as a whole works on a budget of less than $9,000 million a year, including the voluntary funds and the peace-keeping operations, a figure which is not much more than 0.06 per cent of the sum of the budgets of all the Member States. That is roughly what is spent every 15 weeks in Britain on alcohol. It represents less than $2 per human being alive on the planet today, compared with the $150 per capita spent annually by governments on arms and the military.[6]

In 1992, the United Nations workforce, paid for out of the regular budget, consisted of 10,100 people. Counting all the organisations and agencies forming part of the United Nations, the United Nations system has slightly more than 51,000 employees to attend to problems of political negotiation, mediation, food, disarmament, health, development, justice, agriculture, work, culture, children, refugees, etc., all over the world. There is no doubt at all that the bureaucracy in the United Nations is enormous and that another overwhelming necessity is the rationalisation of this gigantic apparatus. But it is also true that the mission and the expectations facing the United Nations system as a whole, whose total workforce is one-fifteenth that of

General Motors, is of a magnitude incomparable to that of any commercial enterprise.

As Galtung has pointed out,[7] the United Nations should be seen as 'the world's public forum', where all the main problems and conflicts can be aired and brought out into the open for all to see and where ideas can be put forward for solving them. What happens in the last instance will depend on the Member States and other non-governmental agencies in the world system. Even the reform of the United Nations itself will depend largely on the pressure that NGOs and social movements bring to bear on their respective governments. After all, if a 'new world order' is to emerge based on co-operation and replacing the 'old order' of the powerful, it can do so only as a result of the commitment and the conspiracy by the planet's civil society to construct everyday experiences of international solidarity. This active participation by the civil society is what is needed if we are to fulfil and even surpass Boutros Boutros-Ghali's *Agenda for Peace*, in itself a good point of departure but not sufficient as a final objective.

The introduction to the United Nations Charter starts with the very words 'We the peoples of the United Nations ...' and not 'we the States' or 'we the governments'. To democratise the process of decision-making it will be necessary to reduce state involvement in the United Nations as far as possible, even if incompletely and gradually, through the active contribution of other agencies and by promoting popular political participation. Improving on the confederal model of the United Nations, based on the theoretical principles of equal sovereignty of states, non-interference in internal affairs and government representation, will be a long and difficult process. The ideal of a voice for all citizens and peoples within the framework of a culture of solidarity and universal citizenship meets with the obstacle of an international reality with many undemocratic governments and with democracies that act according to particular 'reasons of State'.[8]

A first step in this direction could be to recognise new roles for the 831 NGOs which already have consultative status in the United Nations or are associated to its Public Information Department and raising their status from consultative to co-decisional. Although this is obviously not easy to put into practice, due to different traditions in the associative movements and impossibility of holding elections in many countries, I agree with Ravenel's suggestion[9] that state delegations to the General Assembly could have a threefold composition, with an official diplomatic representative (like now), a parliament specially elected by the country's Chamber of Deputies, and a representative chosen by the country's NGOs. A simpler intermediate step but one which would profoundly democratise the United Nations and bring it closer to the public would be to designate a people's representative for each country. Every four years, electors in each country would directly elect someone to represent them on the General Assembly alongside the diplomat designated by the government. In this case each country would have two votes.

The democratisation of the United Nations is, in short, the issue on which all proposals for the organisation's reform should hinge. It must necessarily affect the present system of voting in the General Assembly, which works on the unacceptable principle of 'one country, one vote', without taking into account that some countries have populations ten, a hundred or a thousand times the size of others. It would be fairer and more democratic to find a system which brought voting more into line with this demographic reality, but without going to the extreme of letting a handful of countries control decision-making.

One reasonable proposal is to assign a figure to each country equal to the square root of its population (in millions of inhabitants). Using this formula, the country with the biggest population (China) would have 33 points (or votes), followed by India with 29, the United States with 15, Indonesia with 13 and Brazil and Russia with twelve. Spain would have six points, and 111 countries with populations of less than four million inhabitants would have to make do with one. In this way, the three most populated countries would have just over 12 per cent of the votes, far less than the 42 per cent they would get on the basis of their population, but considerably more than the 1.3 per cent of votes they have at present, a figure which can hardly be called democratic.

Continuing with the previous proposal of appointing at least two representatives per country, one designated by the government and one by popular election, the number of votes per country would automatically be doubled. An even more democratic and representative system would be one that assigned a larger number of representatives to those countries with the largest populations. Thus, for example, those countries with more than 500 million inhabitants would have eight representatives (four appointed by the government and four elected by the people), those with more than 64 million inhabitants would have six, those with more than 25 million would have four, and the rest would have two (one official and one popular).

Two people with a profound understanding of the United Nations, Urquhart and Childers,[10] who to a large extent coincide with and

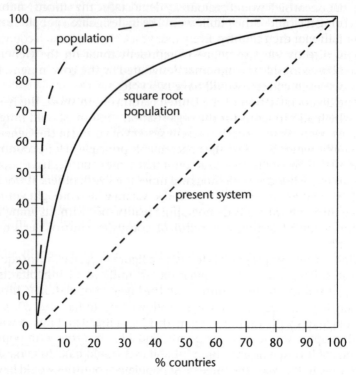

Figure 1.1 Votes/population per country

sum up the ideas put forward in this book, have listed the chief responsibilities of the United Nations system as follows:

- maintenance of early warning systems for possible conflicts and application of preventive diplomacy;
- peace-making, peace-keeping and conflict resolution;
- disarmament, arms regulation and reducing arms flow;
- promotion of an effective system of shared and collective security;
- promotion of a fairer and better orientated management of the world economy;
- proposals for solving the world's financial and monetary problems, including the debt problem;
- mobilising resources and formulating strategies for putting an end to poverty and the marginalisation of the masses;
- leadership in the safeguarding of the environment and in the handling of other matters of a global nature;

- management and improvement of urgent problems, including those raised by refugees and large-scale migrations, natural disasters and other human emergencies, AIDS and the international drug problem;
- co-ordination and improvement of the capacity of the United Nations system for co-operation and development;
- development of and respect for international law in its many new spheres relating to the economy, the environment and social issues, as well as the traditional ones;
- promotion of respect for all human rights and progress in their formulation, with special attention to the elimination of sexual discrimination;
- reinforcing an understanding of the value of cultural diversity and efforts to preserve it;
- fomenting basic innovatory research in support of all this work, including international data banks and multidisciplinary analyses of world trends;
- stimulating participation in the United Nations system by all the components of civil society: citizens and their organisations, employers, academic and research institutions and mass media.

Table 1.1 The square root system: proposal for point assignment for the General Assembly

No.	No. countries	per country	Total
1	China	33	33
1	India	29	29
1	USA	15	15
1	Indonesia	13	13
2	Brazil, Russia	12	24
1	Japan	11	11
3	Nigeria, Pakistan, Bangladesh	10	30
1	Mexico	9	9
2	Germany, Vietnam	8	16
10		7	70
4		6	24
8		5	40
17		4	68
22		3	66
38		2	76
111		1	111
223			635

The United Nations' instructional and educational function is therefore more important than its executive and deterrent function, however significant the latter may be in the future. Educating for peace, co-operation, social equality, coexistence, respect and tolerance, as stated or implied in Article 1 of the Charter, must form the central pillar of the organisation, however difficult this may be for western countries, since amongst other things these values call for a reduction in their material consumption.

Membership of the United Nations should not be an obligation or a routine act. Although universal membership is something to be desired, it is obvious that the advice and decisions of the United Nations will only be valid when Member States accept them simply because they feel they are responsible members of a community. As Galtung has pointed out, 'if a Member State finds this sort of tie unbearable and does not want to be educated in world citizenship, let it go ... it'll be back'.[11]

In the future it would be a good thing to extend the rule that 'anyone who signs an Agreement or Treaty must fulfil it'. This is the idea behind the proposals for the creation of a new Convention on the National and Collective Responsibility of States in Human Rights, as a framework for legitimating possible interventions and making them transparent,[12] and of a Permanent International Court to deal with war crimes, with the capacity to pass judgment on the people responsible for these crimes, something the Court at The Hague cannot at present do. I also agree with Amnesty International's comments on the constitution of the International Court for War Crimes in former Yugoslavia to the effect that 'ad hoc' courts often lack real independence and impartiality and run the risk of being no more than a symbolic gesture to satisfy states' short-term interests. Amnesty International has urged that this court should be the first step towards the construction of a Permanent International Court with the power to pass judgment on serious violations of human rights wherever they take place.[13]

Other Proposals for Change[14]

As well as the changes laid out above and those described in the next chapters on the reform of the Security Council, reinforcement of preventive diplomacy and of the peace-keeping forces, acceptance of the resolutions of the International Court of Justice, etc., the reform of the United Nations includes a long list of measures which can be summed up in the following proposals:

- Regionalisation and decentralisation.

    - Apply the principle of subsidiarity. Anything that can be done on a regional or bilateral level should not be done by the United Nations.[15] Regional conflicts should preferably be solved through regional mechanisms.
    - Reinforce the powers of regional organs, especially in conflict prevention and regulation (a prior step to intervention by the Security Council). These organs would not be able to use force without the consent of the Council. They would need efficient mechanisms for mediation. Conflict-solving committees could also be set up in each region, as well as advisory councils made up of people of recognised standing who could command the respect of the states in the region.
    - As recommended in the Stockholm Initiative,[16] the power of the United Nations peace forces could be significantly increased by the establishment of a network of political agencies of the Secretariat in various countries. These agencies would provide political advice and intermediaries and would promote confidence-building measures.
    - Move the United Nations headquarters to the South, outside the United States.

- Resolve existing obstacles to decision-making.

    - Do away with the right of veto in the Security Council.
    - Grant more autonomy to the Secretary General for deciding and delegating.

- Grant the General Assembly greater capacity for decision-making.

    - This involves reforming Article 12.1 of the Charter[17] so that the General Assembly can make recommendations and influence the decisions of the Security Council.

- Improve and enforce sanctions mechanisms.
- Improve mechanisms for political co-ordination and for consultation between governments and between these and the United Nations.
- Raise the technical level of the political United Nations.[18]

- Organise regular encounters between politicians and experts so that the former can acquire a better understanding of problems.
- Stop using the United Nations as an 'elephant's burial ground' for failed politicians.
- Appoint United Nations officials, including the Secretary General, on professional merit, rather than through personal influence or on criteria of geographical distribution.

• Raise the political level of United Nations experts.

- Greater resolve is needed in dealing with taboo subjects, including the actual reform of the organisation, the right of intervention, etc.

• Reduce the influence of States in the United Nations.

- Increase the role of the NGOs.
- Develop control of United Nations and especially Security Council activities by the NGOs. It would be a good thing if these organisations carried out a detailed control of the resolutions passed by the Council and published an annual report on this.
- Consider the creation of a Second Assembly or People's Chamber as laid down in Article 22.[19]
- Prepare an International Convention on the Right of Peoples to Peace, on the basis of the 1984 United Nations Declaration and including equality of collective rights and the right to self-determination by non-violent legal methods.[20]
- Set up a world service for development, ecology and human rights, linked to the United Nations and substituting military service, in which millions of people could take part.

Reinforcing the United Nations' Finances

As we have already seen, the United Nations works on almost negligible financial resources, with a regular budget of not much more than $1,600 million a year, a paltry sum if we think of the ambitious aims this maximum international organisation has set itself. This budgetary shortage is aggravated by the chronic deficit resulting from some states' traditional reluctance to pay their quotas.

The United Nations' budgetary shortage is also a sign of the general insensitivity towards the chief projects of different UN-linked organisations. Neither the excessive bureaucracy nor even the possible abuses and definite errors in some of these organisations' thinking are an excuse for their lack of determination in tackling international co-operation programmes, inside or outside the United Nations framework, that could restore the dignity of millions of human beings. Once again, we have to remember the feasibility of these projects, at least as regards their financial cost. Three of the most significant programmes in the United Nations system, concerned with food, health and education, have an annual cost of $8,500 million, one per cent of annual expenditure by states on military affairs.

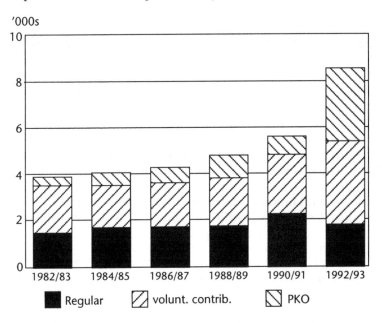

Figure 1.2 The United Nations biennial budget

Table 1.2 Financial cost of some United Nations programmes

$ millions	
1,000	UNICEF programme for preventing child mortality and undernourishment in 50 million children
2,500	WHO programme 'Health for All'
5,000	UNDP–UNESCO programme to ensure that by the year 2000 all children have access to primary schooling

The United Nations regular budget for 1993 was $1,600 million, not much more than the cost for one day of 'Operation Desert Storm' or of a B-2 bomber, less than the consolidated budget of Barcelona City Council for 1993 and similar to the annual budget of the New York City Fire Department. The cost of peace-keeping operations that same year, estimated at some $3,600 million, was less than twice the combined budgets of New York City's Police and Fire departments.[21]

Secretary General Boutros Boutros-Ghali said to the 1994 General Assembly, the United Nations had debts exceeding $1.7 billion at the end of August. It owed $1 billion to Member States for peace-keeping contributions, $400 million to vendors and suppliers, and $325 million for previous budget surpluses. The Organisation needed $400 million each month to cover its costs, but had only $375 million in cash balances. As we can see, the United Nations is bankrupt thanks to the negligence and the express wish of certain states. If we want to strengthen the role of the United Nations, as well as the political health of the organisation, Member States will have to pay their dues on time and in full and will have to agree on a new financial structure so that it can work properly.

Table 1.3 Outstanding contributions to the regular budget for previous years (as at 31 January 1995)

$ (millions)	
United States	212.1
South Africa	57.4
Ukraine	36.4
Former Yugoslavia	9.6
Others	111.7
TOTAL	427.2

The bankruptcy of the United Nations is largely a result of the excessive weight of the United States in its finances. The United States is the principal contributor to United Nations funds, since it supplies no less than 25 per cent of its budget. But it is also the principal defaulter, as a result of which it manages to destabilise or delay the organisation's activity as it pleases.[22]

Japan is the second largest contributor to the regular budget (13.95 per cent), even though it isn't a member of the Security Council. The third largest contributor is Germany, with 8.9 per cent of the budget, and the Russian Federation appears in fifth position, with 5.68 per cent of the budget, and is a traditional defaulter.[23]

Table 1.4 Status of contributions to the United Nations regular budget for 1995

	%	accumulated
United States	25.00	25.00
Japan	13.95	38.95
Germany	8.94	47.89
France	6.32	54.21
Russian Fed.	5.68	59.89
United Kingdom	5.27	65.16
Italy	4.79	69.95
Canada	3.07	73.02
Spain	2.24	75.26
Brazil	1.62	76.88

United Nations finances therefore depend on the goodwill of a very small number of countries, making the institution undemocratic and tremendously vulnerable, since it is a reflection of the economic power of a group of states.

The United Nations system is financed in three ways. There is a regular budget ($1,600 million in 1993) based on the quotas assigned to each state on the basis of its economic wealth.[24] Peace-keeping operations, except for one or two, are financed through contributions by the states, using a scale that reduces the contribution due from the poorest countries.[25] Finally, humanitarian aid and the expenses of the development agencies are covered by voluntary contributions by member countries.

The operation of the United Nations organs and agencies depends largely on the goodwill and generosity of a handful of countries. The international solidarity charts are headed by the four Nordic countries, broadly coinciding with the countries that contribute most to peacekeeping. Although these are rich countries, the voluntary sums they set aside for these organisations far exceed the amount due from them on the basis of their wealth. Other countries, in contrast, although equally wealthy, contribute hardly anything.

Taking as a sample the voluntary contributions, whether of government or private origin, to three significant organs (UNDP, UNICEF and the UNHCR), the five top-ranking countries are as shown in Figure 1.3.

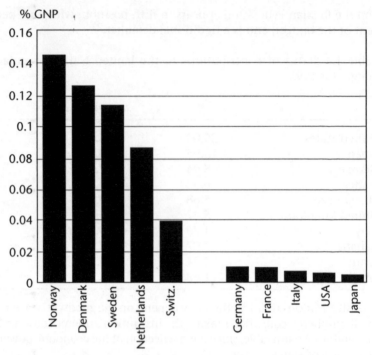

Figure 1.3 1993 contributions UNDP, UNICEF, UNHCR

This classification of voluntary payments is not very different from the figures for official aid to development for the OECD countries, which for 1993 were as follows:

Table 1.5 Public aid to development, 1993 ($ millions)

	Total	*% GNP*	*$ per inhabitant*
Denmark	1,340	1.03	258
Norway	1,014	1.01	234
Sweden	1,769	0.98	203
Netherlands	2,525	0.82	165
France	7,915	0.63	137
Canada	2,373	0.45	83
Finland	355	0.45	70
. . .			
Japan	11,259	0.26	90
USA	9,721	0.15	38

Source: OECD, Rapport CAD 1994.

Although improving the fixed methods of finance (obligatory quotas) is basic to the United Nations' economy, voluntary contributions will obviously continue to play an important role in the future.

To reduce the United Nations' economic dependence on the goodwill of the superpowers, it seems reasonable to set a maximum limit of 15 per cent to Member States' dues, as the Palme Commission pointed out. To make up for the quantitative loss resulting from the reduction in the United States' quota, the size of all the other states' quotas would have to be increased. More than 70 states pay less than $100,000 a year in obligatory dues, and almost two-thirds of the members of the United Nations pay less than $1 million a year, a very small figure if we compare it, for example, with the military expenditure of most of these countries.

Failure to pay the obligatory quotas, an all-too-common occurrence in the organisation, could be solved by withdrawing the right to vote of defaulter states, including of course those in the Security Council. It is not particularly edifying that it should be precisely the permanent members of this council who are most in debt.

To increase the organisation's funds, both the Secretary General and others have proposed various urgent measures, whose appropriateness will have to be discussed during the next few years. Some of these proposals are:

- Establish a reserve fund for peace-keeping operations and a peace reserve of $1,000 million to pay for small operations and the start of other larger ones.[26]
- Allow the United Nations to issue treasury bonds.
- Impose a 1 per cent tax on transport fares, especially airfares, which would go to United Nations funds.
- Set up an international lottery.
- Establish a tax on arms transfers.

In its report on the United Nations' finances, the Ford Foundation came out against these proposals for additional funding on the grounds that governments would have difficulty controlling these amounts and their responsibility in the maintenance of the organisation would be reduced.

Another instructive measure put forward is that the cost of peace-keeping operations should be included in the defence budget rather than the foreign affairs budget. This is, after all, an investment in security,[27] and, as Urquhart points out, an effective peace-keeping system would have the end result of reducing world defence spending.[28] The investment is therefore a wise one.

I agree with the Ford Foundation's observation that the future credibility of the United Nations will depend to a large measure on effective management, the quality of its executive team and the improvement of its structure and administration, including, needless to say, its ability to ensure in good time that it has the necessary funds at its disposal to carry out its obligations. The reform has a definite internal or domestic dimension, without which it will be unable to answer the challenges facing it from the outside.

The renovation of the United Nations, in all its multiple dimensions, is therefore one of the biggest challenges facing the international community as we approach the end of this century. As Archibugi has pointed out,[29] history has shown that the emergence of new institutions (or the in-depth reform of existing institutions) is only possible if there are specific interests working to this end. At this moment, as we shall see in later chapters, there are political and social forces interested in extending the influence and the powers of supranational institutions. Guaranteeing that this possible development in the United Nations is to the benefit of all, and not just a few, is the challenge facing those of us who are not resigned to being mere spectators of the United Nations' transformation.

Proposals

- Analyse and determine the new world context which justifies the existence of an organism such as the United Nations.
- Specify the fields in which the United Nations can act and its priorities.
- Give priority to the policy of conflict prevention, developing early warning systems.
- Pinpoint the purpose of and the differences between humanitarian policies and interventionism.
- Pay special attention to ethnic conflicts, protection of minorities, socio-economic inequalities, ecological issues, disarmament and the achievement of a sustainable development which will put an end to poverty.
- Channel official development aid towards critical spheres of human development.
- Advance the codification and universal acceptance of human rights.
- Demilitarise the concept of security so as to deal with conflicts with the appropriate means and open the way to a system of collective security.

- Transfer power to the United Nations in those areas where simple intergovernmental co-operation is not enough.
- States must commit themselves to follow freely accepted international rules of conduct in which the rights and duties of nations are clearly laid out.
- Find a formula for bringing decision-making more in line with the demographic weight of each country. The square root of the population could indicate the number of votes assigned to each country.
- Establish an effective system of sanctions against countries that fail to fulfil their commitments.
- Set up a Permanent International Court with powers to judge war crimes.
- Reinforce the United Nations' teaching and training role as a forum in which to raise, analyse and channel problems towards positive solutions.
- Stimulate participation in the United Nations system of all the components of civil society, especially the NGOs.
- Recognise new functions for the NGOs which already have a consultative status and raise them to a co-decisional status.
- Promote bi-tripartite delegations to the General Assembly, made up of diplomats, Members of Parliament and NGOs from each country.
- Hold elections in each country every four years to directly elect the people's representatives to the General Assembly.
- Reinforce and clarify the role of the peace-keeping forces.
- Decentralise the United Nations by reinforcing regional organs, especially in their role of conflict prevention.
- Endow the General Assembly with a greater capacity for decision-making.
- Supervision by NGOs of the activities of the different United Nations organs, especially those of the Security Council.
- Increase the obligatory quotas.
- Set a limit on Member States' quotas of 15 per cent of the total budget.
- Withdraw the right to vote of countries who fail to pay their dues.
- Establish a reserve fund of $1,000 million for peace-keeping operations.

2

Enlarging the Security Council

One of the central aspects of the reform of the United Nations is, without doubt, the transformation and enlargement of the Security Council,[1] since today's five permanent members (United States, Russia, France, the United Kingdom and China) are a historical legacy which no longer has any bearing on reality. Some countries, especially Germany and Japan, have openly expressed their wish to join the exclusive club of permanent members. In 1990, the German government suggested the creation of six new permanent members without right of veto (Japan, Germany, Brazil, Egypt, India and Nigeria). Nevertheless, it is yet to be decided what criteria must be followed in deciding who is entitled to this special status.

At the second Conference for a More Democratic United Nations (CAMDUN-2), held in Vienna in September 1991, specific suggestions were made on this issue, as well as more general ones regarding an overall reform of the United Nations. To sum up, the members of CAMDUN proposed extending the Security Council to 18 members, abolishing the right of veto, renaming it the 'Peace and Security Council' and establishing a Permanent Committee of the General Assembly, made up of 15 members representing different geographical areas on a rotational basis, which would watch over the activities of the Council.[2]

Japan and Germany are suitable candidates on account of the economic weight they carry, ranking second and third in the world in this respect, above Russia. In an increasingly interdependent world, it is difficult to exclude these two powers from an organ of political decision-making such as the Security Council, especially when both countries are also among the largest contributors to the United Nations' finances: Japan ranks second and Germany fourth and, what is more, neither of them have debts outstanding.

If we consider large economic powers to be countries with a GNP larger than or close to $1 billion (million million), then as well as the United States, Japan, Germany, Russia, France and the United Kingdom, Italy ought to be amongst the candidates. Its qualifications include the seventh position it has to occupy amongst contributors to United Nations funds and its active participation in the organisation's peace-keeping operations. On the other hand, it would be the fifth European country on the Security Council, which would, of course, be out of all proportion. The idea that it should be the European Community or, even better, the CSCE (now OSCE) who appointed one, two or three representatives to the Council is fairer, would help to reinforce regional organs and therefore be a step towards decentralising the United Nations.

In economic terms, Canada would be the eighth candidate, although it comes well below the countries mentioned above. It is also the eighth contributor to the United Nations. In its favour (and this is something that ought to carry more weight), along with Ireland, it is the country that has taken part in most peace-keeping operations. This fact brings with it a considerable moral authority in the United Nations.

Unless the Security Council is to become a political expression of the club of the top economic powers, the demographic weight of nations is the other important factor to be taken into account in the debate on the enlargement of the Security Council. This especially affects India, a country whose population represents 16 per cent of humanity. This alone makes it difficult to exclude it from the Security Council.

Of the ten countries with more than 100 million inhabitants, half of them would be entitled to a place on the Security Council under the criteria listed so far. These are China, India, Russia, the United States and Japan. The other five are, in order of population, Indonesia, Brazil, Nigeria, Bangladesh and Pakistan. Should any of them occupy a seat on the Security Council?

Of the Asian countries, Indonesia would be the only possible candidate, although its low economic level (its GNP is half that of South Korea, for example) and its disregard of civil and political rights detract from its suitability beside other candidates. In any case, this fourth candidate reduces the chances for Bangladesh and Pakistan.

Africa, on the other hand, only has Nigeria to offer as a country with a large population, even double that of Egypt, the second African state in terms of population. But Nigeria is not even the country with most economic resources. Both Egypt and Algeria carry more economic weight in the continent, a fact which complicates the choice. In this case, the best formula might be that of regional representation through the OAU, unless one accepted Nigeria and Egypt, representing black Africa and the Arab world, respectively.

It could also be said that the Arab world should have a permanent member appointed by the Arab League, so long as this organisation acted more in keeping with the spirit and the affairs of the United Nations.

In Latin America, Brazil is the country with most likelihood of joining a new Security Council. It ranks sixth in the world in population and tenth in GNP, far ahead of any other Latin-American country. Mexico would be the second candidate. However, if Latin America were to have two representatives on the Council, the fairest arrangement would be to include one from Brazil and one elected by the OAS.

There remains the possibility of including the Middle East as a region, though no one would question the difficulty of finding a candidate who did not put backs up in some countries in the area. Iran would be the most suitable candidate, in terms both of population and of economic weight, but this would only make sense in the framework of a regional agreement on security, disarmament and co-operation yet to be invented. The present situation rules out this possibility.

One thing which up till now has had a lot to do with the immobility of the Security Council is the fact that the countries making it up all possess nuclear arms. Nuclear power has been a synonym for political power. But in the new plan for the future, the possession of nuclear arms should be considered an obstacle, not a virtue, for anyone wanting a seat on the Council which, amongst its other missions, must encourage disarmament and denuclearisation of the planet. The new nuclear or quasi-nuclear powers (India, South Africa, Israel, Pakistan and a few more) should not only not make use of this strength to press their candidacy, they should cancel their nuclear projects if they aspire to occupying a seat.

The Security Council of the year 2000 should bear no resemblance to the Security Council of the Cold War, or even to today's. Ideally, it should be formed by those countries which in the last decades have shown the greatest commitment to the objectives of the United Nations programmes; that is, security, disarmament, co-operation and human rights. In this case, all the Nordic countries (Sweden, Finland, Norway and Denmark), along with Canada, Ireland and Holland, are more entitled to give advice and take decisions than any of the superpowers. Nevertheless, and in spite of the fact that Article 23.1 of the Charter states that, in electing non-permanent members, 'due regard [will be] specially paid, in the first instance to the contribution of members of the United Nations to the maintenance of international peace and security and to the other purposes of the Organization', in view of the difficulty of reorganising the Council on the basis of this legitimating principle, it would not be a bad idea to remember this if the OSCE ever had to decide who to send as its representatives. Even if it never gets a chance to be put into practice, I find Richard Falk's suggestion that a permanent place be reserved on the Security Council for a 'moral superpower' elected by a panel of Nobel Peace Prize winners very edifying.[3]

This criterion was also used by the Spanish Foreign Affairs Minister, Javier Solana, in his speech to the United Nations General Assembly on 30 September 1993, when he proposed a new category of non-permanent members who would have a place on the Security Council more frequently than other countries, on the basis of their contribution to international peace and security; in other words, to the stipulations of Article 23 mentioned above.

There are, therefore, various formulas that could be used to change the composition of the Security Council. One would be to include, as well as the five present members, eight more who stand out for their economic or demographic status and which would affect the countries shown in Table 2.1.

Table 2.1 Formula for composition of the Security Council (1)

Present members	Economic weight	Demographic weight
United States	Japan	India
Russia	Germany	Indonesia
China	Italy	Brazil
United Kingdom	Canada	Nigeria
France		

A Permanent Council made up in this way would include five representatives from the Third World and eight from the First, a far more balanced proportion than the present 1 to 4, but with Africa and Latin America barely represented as compared to the overwhelming Euro-Asian predominance. Furthermore, countries with a similar level of population to Nigeria, such as Bangladesh and Pakistan, might be tempted to stimulate their already high rate of population growth so as to qualify for entry to the club, something which would obviously be counterproductive.

A second proposal would be to set the number of permanent members at eleven, following more geographical criteria and introducing representatives of regional organisations. The two great military powers, the United States and Russia, would be guaranteed their present seats on the basis of their economic and demographic weight. China would be entitled to a seat on the significant grounds of representing more than one-fifth of the world's population, as would India for similar reasons of population. Japan, which controls 15 per cent of the world's GNP, could not be excluded either. On the other hand, France, the United Kingdom and Germany, which form part of the EC and the OSCE, could take turns in a quota of seats assigned to the OSCE, one of which would be reserved for them. Italy has already suggested that France and the United Kingdom should take a joint EC seat, which is much the same as the proposal above. There is still the question of whether Brazil, with its immense weight in Latin America, could also occupy a permanent seat on the Security Council, while the second seat would be for a country appointed by the OAS. In Africa, where there is no one country that leads the continent in any sense, the two representatives could be chosen by the OAU, and perhaps also by the Arab League. This would give rise to the following composition:

Table 2.2 Formula for composition of Security Council (2)

United States	1	Brazil	1
Russia	1	OAS	1
OSCE	2		
China	1	Arab League	1
India	1	OAU	1
Japan	1		

Under this arrangement, the North–South balance would be improved, and every continent except Oceania would be represented by at least two members.

Whatever the formula used to elect members to the Security Council, what is certain is that they must have the legitimacy to impose sanctions on any country not complying with the Council's resolutions. However, there are serious doubts as to whether or not its composition could carry this moral authority. A few significant figures, though, should clear up these doubts.

Of the 13 countries referred to in the first proposal, only five (United Kingdom, Japan, Canada, India and Nigeria) have made declarations recognising the jurisdiction of the International Court of Justice as binding. The other eight do not accept its rulings as binding.[4] With this state of affairs, how can the Council recommend or oblige conflicting parties to submit themselves to the jurisdiction of this high court?

Another interesting figure concerns arms trading by this group of countries. The present five permanent members are also the world's leading exporters of heavy weaponry. Germany ranks third, Italy ninth and Czechoslovakia seventh. How can these countries be responsible for the control and reduction of arms movements if they themselves are the chief instigators of this activity? How can they promote disarmament when six of them have nuclear weapons and the 13 countries put together have a total of twelve million soldiers?

Table 2.3 Arms exporting countries and the Security Council

Exporters (1989–1993)	Security Council status
1 United States	permanent member
2 Russia	permanent member
3 Germany	non-permanent member (1995–1996) and candidate for permanent membership
4 France	permanent member
5 United Kingdom	permanent member
6 China	permanent member
7 Czechoslovakia	non-permanent member (1994–1995)
8 Netherlands	…
9 Italy	non-permanent member (1995–1996) and candidate for permanent membership
10 Israel	…

Source: *SIPRI Yearbook 1994*, p. 484.

The countries belonging to the Security Council, both permanent members and others, have yet to sign a large number of treaties and pacts on human rights. Of the nine existing juridical instruments touching on the matter, the United States has yet to sign eight, China four and the United Kingdom three. The permanent members have yet to sign more than a third of these treaties and pacts, a proportion not very different from that corresponding to the 20 non-permanent members of the Council during 1993, 1994 and 1995.

Amongst these, Djibouti, Oman, Botswana and Indonesia stand out for having signed only one or two, followed by Pakistan, Japan and Honduras, with three agreements signed in September 1993. With such glaring contradictions, how can the Security Council encourage or oblige respect for and fulfilment of rights in the world?

These questions lead us into the realms of political fiction which, while unrealistic, is nevertheless highly instructive as the place in which to consider the rules and conditions for admission to the Security Council. These conditions could include that applicants must:

- be fully paid up with the United Nations;
- have signed and ratified the chief agreements on disarmament and human rights;
- respect the rulings of the International Court of Justice;
- devote less than 3 per cent of their GNP to military expenditure;
- take part in the United Nations peace forces; and
- have fulfilled all the Security Council resolutions affecting them.

Imposing conditions for membership of the Security Council is not frivolous or an attempt to prevent certain specific countries from taking part. It is simply a basic condition for endowing this organ with a legitimacy it has not had up to now. The Council can only take decisions affecting the international community if it acts coherently, responsibly and with moral authority. So-called 'world governance' must on no account depend on the military might of a superpower with mercenary leanings, but on the ability of the Security Council, and especially of the permanent members, to exact respect for the rules of conduct approved by the United Nations, by whatever means necessary, but always from a position of legitimacy conferred on them by their own compliance to these rules.

As for non-permanent members, the present formula of ten members for a two-year period, with five members renewed each year, could continue. In this way, the Security Council would be made up of a total of 23 or 21 members according to the formula chosen, with the permanent members slightly outnumbering the non-permanent members.

Needless to say, non-permanent membership would also be subject to certain prior conditions. The lack of legitimacy I referred to in speaking of the five present members with right of veto also affects several of the ten non-permanent countries on the Security Council in 1993 or 1994 (Japan, Venezuela, Hungary, Cape Verde, Morocco, Brazil, Pakistan, Spain, New Zealand and Djibouti in 1993. In 1994 the first five were replaced by Argentina, Oman, Nigeria, Rwanda and the Czech Republic). Let us look at some examples.

In October 1993, apart from the United States and Russia which are permanent members, five of the ten non-permanent countries on the Security Council (Venezuela, Morocco, Cape Verde, Brazil and Djibouti) had payments outstanding of $355 million to the United Nations regular budget, and nine of the 15 countries owed dues to peace-keeping operations (PKOs) carried out in previous years. Of the five which joined in 1994, three (Nigeria, Argentina and Rwanda) were behind in their payments to the regular budget and three

Table 2.4 The Security Council and human rights

	CESCR	CCPR	OPI	OPI2	CERD	APAR	CEDAW	CAT	CRC
United States	no		no	no	no	no	no	no	no
Russia				no					
France				no		no			
United Kingdom			no	no		no			
China	no	no	no	no					
1992–1993									
Japan			no	no	no	no		no	no
Venezuela									
Hungary				no					
Cape Verde			no	no	no				
Morocco			no	no		no			
1993–1994									
Brazil			no	no		no			
Pakistan	no	no	no	no			no	no	
Spain						no			
N–Zealand						no			
Djibouti	no	no	no	no	no	no	no	no	
1994–1995									
Argentina				no					
Oman	no	no	no	no	no		no	no	no
Nigeria			no	no				no	
Rwanda			no	no				no	
Czech Republic				no					
1995–1996									
Germany						no			
Italy				no		no			
Indonesia	no	no	no	no	no	no		no	
Botswana	no	no	no	no		no	no	no	no
Honduras		no	no	no	no	no		no	

Key:

CESCR   International covenant on economic, social and cultural rights.
CCPR   International covenant on civil and political rights.
OPI   Optional protocol to the international covenant on civil and political rights.
OPI2   Second optional protocol to the international covenant on civil and political rights aimed at the abolition of capital punishment.
CERD   International convention on the elimination of all forms of racial discrimination.
APAR   International convention on the suppression and punishment of the crime of apartheid.
CEDAW Convention on the elimination of all forms of discrimination against women.
CAT   Convention against torture and other cruel, inhuman or degrading forms of treatment or punishment.
CRC   Convention on the rights of the child.

Source: United Nations, *Statut des instruments internationaux relatifs au droits de l'homme au 1 septembre 1993*, Geneva, 15 September 1993.

(Czech Republic, Argentina and Rwanda) had debts outstanding from PKOs.

But there is more to come. In January 1994, three countries, Argentina, Brazil and Pakistan, had not signed the Non-Proliferation Treaty; Venezuela, the Antarctic Treaty; Morocco had not ratified the BW Convention; Japan, the Treaty of Rarotonga, and eight countries had not signed the Inhumane Weapons Convention. Oman, which joined the Council in 1994, has hardly signed or ratified a single agreement on disarmament, excepting the BW Convention. Indonesia, Botswana and Honduras, three new non-permanent members in 1995, had not signed the Enmod Convention and the Inhumane Weapons Convention.[5] Furthermore, the 15 non-permanent countries during the two-year period 1993–4 bought heavy armaments to a value of over $24,000 million in the five years 1988–92. Curiously enough, 90 per cent of this armament was sold by the five permanent members, which goes to show how difficult it is to reduce this deadly trade, following the example of our supposed mentors in disarmament.

Of the ten non-permanent members during 1993 or 1994, three (Oman, Morocco and Pakistan) maintain a very high level of military expenditure, both as a proportion of GNP and of the total national budget. The Czech Republic, Spain and Brazil, though to a lesser degree than the five permanent members, also rank amongst the arms exporters. In short, a poor example to set.

It is not yet clear whether the right of veto is maintained for some countries and whether permanent membership is indefinite in all cases or for a fixed period of time to be decided. Since both the demographic and economic criteria used in gauging a country's status undergo changes, we could consider a temporary period of, for example, ten years for the new permanent members, which would be eight countries in the first option and seven in the second. Every ten years, therefore, the composition of this Council would be revised. A proposal of this nature has been made by the United Nations Association of the United States, which suggests that permanent members should not be perpetual, but subject to periodic renewal on the basis of previously defined criteria, such as their financial contribution to the United Nations, their contribution to the peace-keeping forces or their total population.

Regarding the right of veto of the five countries which at present hold this privilege, the aim ought to be its definitive abolition before the year 2000. In the meantime the five permanent members should commit themselves to not using this right, so as to get the new mechanisms greased. At all events, it is very strange that these five countries should not be able to adopt any kind of joint action directed against the interests of any of them.[6]

With the right of veto abolished, and with 23 or 21 members on the Council, decision-making can never be made to depend on unanimous agreement. A majority of three-quarters ought to be enough, leaving a margin of five dissenting voices in the two options discussed.

Table 2.5 World candidate checklist (*)

	Pop.	*GNP*	*UN quota*	*No. PKF*	*No. PKO*	*Accept. ICJ*
China	1	11				N
India	2	13		3	12	Y
United States	3	1	1	7	17	N
Indonesia	4			18		N
Brazil	5	10	10			N
Russia	6	9	3	21	14	N
Japan	7	2	2			Y
Nigeria	8				12	Y
Pakistan	9			1		Y
Bangladesh	10			4	6	N
Mexico	11	16				Y
Germany	12	3	4	15		N
Italy	16	5	7	6	6	N
United Kingdom	17	6	6	5		Y
France	19	4	5	2	17	N
Canada		7	8	9	2	Y
Spain		8	9	22	25	Y

(*) The rank occupied is only mentioned when it stands out in the international context

Key:
GNP   Gross National Product
PKF   Peace-keeping Forces
PKO   Peace-keeping Operations
ICJ   International Court of Justice

Article 24 of the United Nations Charter confers on the Security Council 'primary responsibility for the maintenance of international peace and security' and Article 25 states that United Nations Members 'agree to accept and carry out the decisions of the Security Council'.

But the responsibility and the commitment the members of the Council acquire regarding the international community is also included in the following article, Article 26, not widely publicised on account of its compromising nature, since it points out that:

> in order to promote the establishment and maintenance of international peace and security with the least diversion for armaments of the world's human and economic resources, the Security Council shall be responsible for formulating ... plans ... for the establishment of a system for the regulation of armaments.

The commitment to peace and security, in the widest sense is, according to the Charter, what legitimates the Security Council. Until very recently, the permanent members of the Council have been responsible for rearmament and international militarisation – in other words, the opposite. The challenge as we turn the century is therefore to return to the principles expressed in the Charter, with a structure, composition and working of the Security Council which can guarantee that its members will not behave in a way which is clearly incompatible with their role as instigators of a worldwide security policy.

Proposals

- Increase the number of permanent members to 11 or 13.
- Increase the presence of Third World countries.
- Introduce the presence of regional organisations (OSCE, OAU, OAS, etc.).
- Within the OSCE, guarantee a place for France, the United Kingdom and Germany on a rotational basis.
- A temporary period of ten years for new permanent countries.
- Abolish the right of veto by the year 2000.
- Maintain the present structure of ten non-permanent members sitting for a two-year period.
- Lay down conditions for membership of the Council:

  - be fully paid up with the UN;
  - accept the International Court of Justice;
  - take part in the United Nations Peace Forces;
  - fulfil the Council's resolutions;
  - sign agreements on disarmament and human rights.

- Decisions by a three-quarters majority.

THE SECURITY COUNCIL AND CURRENT CONFLICTS
(involvement between 1993 and 1994)

AFGHANISTAN
   Conflict between the government and hostile groups. More than
   2,000 dead during 1993. Hundreds dead in the capital during the
   first six month of 1994. More than 600,000 people have fled from
   the Kabul area.

ALGERIA
   Conflict between the government and fundamentalist groups (FIA
   and GIA). More than 30,000 dead.

ANGOLA
   Conflict between the government and UNITA. Peace agreements
   broken. Air raids on civilian population. More than 200,000 dead
   since 1990, at least 20,000 of them during 1993.

   PEACE-KEEPING OPERATION (UNAVEM II). Embargo on arms
   and oil. Precarious peace agreement.

AZERBAIJAN
   Conflict with Armenia over the territory of Nagorno-Karabakh,
   situated inside Azerbaijan. More than 1,000 dead during 1993.

   Resolutions requesting the withdrawal of occupying troops.
   (CSCE observer mission).

BOSNIA
   Territorial conflict between the government and Croatian and
   Serbo–Bosnian military forces.

   PEACE-KEEPING OPERATION (UNPROFOR). Use of air force.
   Strengthening of sanctions against Bosnian Serb forces.

BURUNDI
   Conflict between Hutus and Tutsis, between government and
   army, and between army and Rwandan refugees. More than 100,000
   dead since October 1993. Attemps to overthrow government
   (October 1993 and April 1994). Assassinations of President (October
   1993) and Chief of State (April 1994).

   Fact-finding mission.

CAMBODIA
Conflict between government and Khmer Rouge, before and after the election of May 1993.

PEACE-KEEPING OPERATION (UNTAC) until the end of 1993.

CHECHENIA
Conflict between government of General Dudáviev and armed opposition supported by Russia.

COLOMBIA
Conflict between government and guerrilla movements (FARC and ELN). More than 20,000 dead since 1986. Widespread violence. 1,500 dead during 1993.

CROATIA
Conflict between government and Serb forces.

PEACE-KEEPING OPERATION (UNPROFOR).

CUBA
Conflict between the government and the political opposition. Thousands of people escape on rafts towards US.

GAMBIA
Military coup in July 1994.

GEORGIA
Conflict between government and opposition. Territorial conflict over Abkhazia. Ethnic cleansing. More than 2,000 dead since 1993. More than 300,000 refugees or displaced people.

PEACE-KEEPING OPERATION (UNOMIG). Fact-finding mission on ethnic cleansing. Mediation by Russia. CSCE Mission since December 1992. South Ossetia Joint Force since July 1992.

HAITI
Military coup in September 1991. The rebels have not kept to the agreements of July 1993. Thousands of Haitians flee in boats towards US.

PEACE-KEEPING OPERATION (UNMIH) frustated. General embargo. Military intervention by USA.

INDIA
Territorial conflicts with various rebel groups. More than 20,000 dead during 1993.

INDONESIA
Conflict between the government and the population of East Timor, annexed by force in 1975. More than 20,000 dead since then.

IRAN
Territorial conflict between government and mujahideen. Territorial conflict with the Kurds.

IRAQ
Government conflict with Kurds and with pro-Iranian Muslims. Border conflict with Kuwait.

PEACE-KEEPING OPERATION (UNIKOM) on the border. Resolutions on the demarcation of the border with Kuwait, payment of compensation to Iraqi citizens and withdrawal of troops deployed along the border.

ISRAEL
Territorial conflict with Lebanon and with Palestinians.

Resolution condemning attacks by Jewish settlers. International mediation to negotiate peace with Palestinians.

LEBANON
Conflict with Israel. Air raids by Israel.

PEACE-KEEPING OPERATION (UNIFIL).

LIBERIA
Conflict between government and NPFL. More than 20,000 dead in four years of war, almost 2,000 of them during 1993.

PEACE-KEEPING OPERATION (UNOMIL). Arms embargo. ECOWAS cease-fire monitoring since August 1990.

LIBYA
Conflict with Security Council over supposed support by Libyan government to terrorist groups.

Air and financial embargo. Observer mission (UNASOG) for Libyan withdrawal from the Aozou region.

MACEDONIA
Conflict with the Federal Republic of Yugoslavia.

PEACE-KEEPING OPERATION (UNPROFOR) CSCE Mission since September 1992.

MEXICO
Conflict between government and Chiapas guerrilla movement.

MOZAMBIQUE
Conflict between government and RENAMO. More than one million dead and five million refugees and displaced people since 1976.

PEACE-KEEPING OPERATION (ONUMOZ).

MYANMAR
Conflict between government and opposition. Territorial conflict in Karen.

NIGER
Territorial conflict with FLAA.

NIGERIA
Conflict between military government and opposition.

NORTHERN IRELAND
Conflict between British government and IRA.

Cease-fire agreement prior to negotiations in 1994.

NORTH KOREA
Conflict between government and IAEA over nuclear inspections.

Threats of sanctions. Mediation by US.

PERU
Conflict between government and Shining Path/MRTA. More than 1,000 dead during 1993.

PHILIPPINES
Conflict between government and guerrilla movements (NPA and MNFL). Territorial conflict in Mindanao. More than 500 dead during 1993.

RWANDA
Conflict between government and FPR. Conflict between Hutu extremists and Tutsi/Hutu opposition. Genocide. Half a million dead between April and August 1994. More than two million refugees.

PEACE-KEEPING OPERATIONS (UNOMUR–UNAMIR). French military intervention. US military presence. Creation of International Tribunal.

SAHARA
Conflict between Morocco and Frente Polisario.

PEACE-KEEPING OPERATION (MINURSO).

SOMALIA
Conflict between clans.

PEACE-KEEPING OPERATION (UNOSOM). US military intervention (Unified Task Force). Use of force.

SOUTH AFRICA
Conflict between rival groups. More than 4,000 dead during 1993.

PEACE-KEEPING OPERATION (UNOMSA) until June 1994.

SUDAN
Conflict between Muslim government and Christian and animist population in the south. Ethnic cleansing of Nubas. Territorial conflict with SPLA/SPLM factions. One million people may have died in the last ten years.

TAJIKISTAN
Conflict between pro-Russian Popular Front and the alliance formed by democrats and Christians. More than 16,000 dead during 1993.

United Nations mediation. CSCE mission since December 1993. CIS Tajikistan Buffer Force since March 1993. UNITED NATIONS MISSION OF OBSERVERS (UNMOT) in December 1994.

TURKEY
Conflict between government and Kurds (PKK). More than 3,000 militants dead in 1994.

YEMEN
Civil war between North and South in 1994. More than 7,000 dead.

Fact-finding mission. US mediation.

YUGOSLAVIA (Federal Republic)
Conflict with Bosnia and Croatia.

General embargo and sanctions. European Community Monitoring Mission since July 1991.

3

Conflict Prevention

As the name itself indicates, the basic purpose of conflict prevention is to take the right action at the first signs of conflict and keep it from crossing a certain threshold beyond which it can easily get out of control. If the conflict is dealt with in the early stages – that is, when it first shows itself – it can be properly regulated. Prevention, therefore, consists in detecting it in time and dealing with it correctly. As it is always difficult to stop a conflict once it has started, the best thing is not to let it reach bursting point and get out of control.

To carry this out, the first thing that is needed is the ability to predict the course of events. This calls for accurate information, which will allow a correct analysis and warn observers when a conflict is beginning to reach a dangerous level.

Early Warning Centres

Like the part played by AWACS aircraft in aerial strategy, the expression 'early warning' is used both in diplomacy and in conflict regulation to refer to systems which tell us of the existence of crisis situations. Thus an advance warning on human rights violations and violent conflicts refers to measures which serve to prevent the apparition of flagrant violations of these rights, at the same time providing the mechanisms for more efficient conflict regulation.

If it is to be effective, a preventive policy must take into account not only questions of strictly military security,[1] but also political, economic, ecological, social, cultural and technological matters that also belong in the field of security. Each of these spheres can have its own early warning systems to inform of problems as they arise, so that they can be dealt with in time.

We live in a world with a wide variety of conflicts, which are a result of poverty, borders, nationalism, migrations,[2] destruction of the environment, militarism and many other factors, which are not always sufficiently closely monitored for us to be able to forecast their capacity for destabilisation, especially when they have a planetary scope. Unfortunately, in most cases, we only start to act when the problem affects the interests of the more powerful nations, without a truly collective security system being put into operation on a global or universal scale.

Recognising this diversity in conflicts is essential to reorienting security policies which have traditionally centred on an analysis of military threats, whether real or imagined. The militarisation of security has prevented attention to highly lethal conflicts such as ethnic or ecological conflicts or those resulting from natural catastrophes. During the 1980s, conflicts resulting from natural catastrophes affected 64 million people, most of them inhabitants of the Third World,[3] Gurr has catalogued and analysed 40 genocides and politicides since the Second World War,[4] 39 of which have also taken place in the Third World, producing an 'ethnoclass' of tens of millions of refugees on the run from civil wars and repression.

It is therefore only natural that, in designing a policy of prevention and in its plans for a peace force, the United Nations should pay special attention to the care of refugees, resolving ethnic conflicts and the creation of 'green helmets' for ecological conflicts.[5] The existence of nuclear power stations in bad repair or without any kind of security system, for example, is an obvious case of a global security threat of a non-military nature which similarly can only be solved by non-military means.[6] The list of ecological problems could go on to include conflicts over water (dams and lakes, river courses, excessive salinity, soil erosion, etc.), fisheries (including piracy), agricultural land, toxic waste, chemical pollution, deforestation, acid rain, etc.[7]

Preventive diplomacy, however, involves overcoming the present reluctance to attend to the causes of foreseeable catastrophes, and, as many analysts point out, among them Bertrand:

> unfortunately, it is not difficult to foresee that the disintegration taking place in many countries will also lead to catastrophes. Now is the time to avoid an explosion of 'new Yugoslavias'. When the catastrophe has been unleashed, it will obviously be too late. It is not beyond our means to define methods of prevention. It is no secret to anyone that what pushes groups of people desirous of the decent life they deserve and the recognition of their identity to take refuge in tribal hatred, fundamentalism, dictatorial powers or emigration abroad are situations of extreme poverty, of marginalisation or of desperation.[8]

To solve these conflicts, what is needed is a new mentality, one prepared to approach problems in a proper, responsible manner and capable of creating adequate means for resolving them. An ethnic conflict, for example, should never be approached or resolved in the same way as a conventional war between states. In this sort of conflict, the role of the United Nations should perhaps be keeping open the possibility of reaching a political agreement,[9] or of warning of the risks resulting from the existence of economically very run-down regions in a multi-ethnic area.[10] The treatment of ecological conflicts, to give another example, calls for attention to the habitat destroyed as well as to the resulting refugees, something which at present lies outside the traditional functions of military institutions.

One example of a non-military advance warning system is the FAO's Global Information and Early Warning System (GIEWS). Its mission consists in foreseeing the effects of factors such as adverse weather conditions, variations in crop sizes, fluctuations in prices, market behaviour and government policies affecting food production. It also takes into account the needs of refugees and displaced people. In Africa, the GIEWS completes its work with satellite surveillance of the vegetation.[11]

The preventive work of the early warning centres can take place in different ambits (national, regional and international) and institutions (governmental or non-governmental). Prediction and prevention can be carried out through the United Nations, through regional institutions (OSCE, EC, NATO, WEU) or through Ministries of Defence or Foreign Affairs.

To be effective, an early warning system must work at various levels at the same time, thus ensuring that conflicts are detected from one or more of these levels. The United Nations, as the maximum international organ, is at the top. The networks of social movements and the NGOs are at the bottom, nearest the people. The intermediate levels are occupied by regional and state organisations.

The decentralisation or federalisation of the United Nations, which is one of the aspects awaiting reform, would be a useful contribution to the task of prevention since it would make it possible to establish early warning systems in all the regional organisations associated with the United Nations. It has been suggested that Commissions for Security and Confidence Creation (CSC) be set up,[12] whose job it would be to identify potential sources of conflict in the region and alert the United Nations system, develop positive approaches for preventing conflicts, take active steps to solve them, set confidence-creating measures in motion, preserve the inviolability of borders, establish agreements for the non-implementation of force, provide security for small states, etc.

The Charter of Paris for a new Europe, signed on 21 November 1990, established the creation of a Conflict Prevention Centre (CPC) based in Vienna, as a way of reducing conflicts in Europe. The work of this valuable CSCE centre consists in favouring the application of measures to promote trust and security; for example, through mechanisms for consultation and co-operation in matters of military activities, establishing a communications network, co-operation in cases of dangerous accidents of a military nature or preparing seminars on military doctrines.

However, the CPC started life with severe limitations to its sphere of action. Although the Charter of Paris itself states that the CPC 'could take on other functions, such as reconciliation and settling of disputes', at present no one seems to want to give it the necessary facilities or means for it to be anything more than just an administrative and bureaucratic office. With a tiny full-time staff and a negligible budget, it is extremely significant that the Centre's first director should have said, on the very day of its inauguration, that 'any mediation activity in conflicts within states, such as that taking place in Yugoslavia, is out of the question'.

The best thing would be to achieve close co-operation between all the levels mentioned so far, so as to create a global communications network between all the early warning centres, which, in the interests of efficiency, should use the same computer language and standardise their treatment of the information received. Whatever the case, rapid communication is of vital importance in the work of the early warning systems, as well as a capacity to rapidly publicise the facts concerning a critical situation, independent of the fact that it is sometimes best to fall back on 'silent diplomacy' in dealing with certain conflicts.

In this respect it could be extremely useful to create an international network of labour associations, legal aid organisations and humanitarian, ecological and human rights movements, such as Amnesty International, Red Cross, International Peace Brigades, Médecins Sans Frontières, churches, trade unions, alternative press agencies, UNHCR, UNICEF, UNESCO, UNDP, Greenpeace and a long list of other groups and institutions, united in a noble alliance to promote the dignity of peoples.

With a network of this sort, in which a significant role would be played by the NGOs of Third World countries, it would be possible to analyse conflict situations between states – often the starting point for conflicts which go on to affect entire regions – with more rigour and precision; in other words, with more possibilities of prevention.

Obviously, the policy of prevention cannot be limited simply to identifying the problem; it must help find the right way to treat it and solve it. It must also allow rapid action in the face of emergency situations, linking the work of surveillance to the response. The early warning must therefore be accompanied by an advance commitment when the situation demands it,[13] instead of the traditional military concept of 'early defence':

> Permanent political agencies in key regions, military observation teams, fact-finding missions and collective security forces could constitute a global emergency system, a kind of 'global surveillance' which could be deployed before confrontations get violent.[14]

The in-depth treatment of conflicts is not, however, exclusively a job for the United Nations, nor even its principal task. It is preferably the responsibility of governments, peoples and the social fabric. The role of the United Nations is more modest, but indispensable: to detect problems, conflicts and trends, suggest ways of solving conflicts and provide the framework in which to discuss both problems and solutions.

Verification Centres

The job of the early warning systems must be linked to that of the organs that verify and watch over arms agreements. This is also preventive work, since monitoring and verification help preserve trust between the parties to an agreement or a commitment, whether this refers to arms control, a cease-fire, demilitarisation, neighbourliness, the arms trade or avoiding dangerous military deployments.

In 1988, the members of the Six Nations Initiative (Argentina, Greece, India, Mexico, Sweden and Tanzania) proposed that a Commission of the United Nations General Assembly carry out a study on the establishment of a United Nations Verification Agency (UNVA). Amongst the arguments put forward in support of this move, the most important ones concern the financial saving (the upkeep of a single agency in charge of watching over all the agreements is cheaper than an infrastructure for each one), speed (the existence of one agency would mean that a team of people specially trained for this work could be on permanent alert), confidentiality (it is easier to report treaty violations to an organ depending on the United Nations), trust (countries can trust in the impartiality and objectivity of the Secretary General) and the retrospective range (an organ of this sort could verify old treaties which had not foreseen this type of measure at the time of signing). According to a United Nations study, the cost of setting up and operating an agency of this sort would amount to some $1,000 million.

For the United Nations, and especially for the Secretary General, it is essential to have sufficient viable information. To obtain this, it has often been proposed that the United Nations should have its own monitoring apparatus, including the information obtained from satellites.[15] In this connection, the Palme Commission report, mentioned above, states that 'certain advanced technologies, such as seismic and acoustic sensors, mobile radars, advanced communications methods, and even aerial surveillance systems, could contribute in different ways to the surveillance of cease-fires and separation zones'. As Renner,[16] Johansen[17] and other analysts have pointed out in stressing the United Nations' need for greater independence and information-gathering capacity, the possibility must be seriously considered that the United Nations should have an International Satellite Control Agency, which along with other, complementary means (reconnaissance aircraft and other forms of observation) would provide impartial information in support of preventive diplomacy (foreseeing surprise attacks, troop movements, treaty violations, cease-fire controls, treaty verification, aid to peace-keeping missions, etc.).

Although the advantages of an agency of this sort are obvious, it is nevertheless surprising that it would be competing with military satellites belonging to the countries that at present are permanent members of the Security Council. The most appropriate, or at least the most economical step would be to establish an agreement by which some of these satellites were transferred to other missions and passed into the hands of the United Nations, and that specialised personnel belonging to the Organisation should be in charge of handling them and interpreting the images.

The United Nations and Conflict Prevention

The United Nations Charter, Article 1, states quite clearly that the Organisation's activities must preferably be preventive and that its purpose must be to prevent conflicts breaking out rather than to intervene in ending them.

> The Purposes of the United Nations are:
> 1. To maintain international peace and security, and to that end: to take effective collective measures for the prevention and removal of threats to the peace ...

In spite of this, the United Nations has not up to now been capable of efficient action in the field of prevention, whether because of the lack of collaboration between countries, the lack of adequate mechanisms or resources or the obstacles put in its way by the permanent members of the Security Council during the long period of the Cold War. Moreover, there is sensitivity among developing states about the possibility of the United Nations using 'intelligence' about them to their detriment, and there is opposition to United Nations intelligence-gathering capabilities because of more amorphous concern about the United Nations becoming the precursor of an all-seeing, all knowing world government.[18] It has been traditional to call on the services of the United Nations to intervene in the final stages of a conflict or at a moment when all hopes of solving it have been lost. This marginal, after-the-event role of the United Nations is the opposite of the preventive function assigned to it.

The failure of the United Nations to take preventive action has been brought up and criticised over and over again by different Secretary Generals. Nevertheless, things began to change in 1993 with the start of courses in Austria for international and civil servants on peace-making and preventive diplomacy, and because in 1992–3 more fact-finding missions were despatched than in any previous such period in the United Nations' history. In his annual report for 1982, Pérez de Cuéllar asked for greater systematic powers to be developed for direct investigation in potential areas of conflict. In 1989, he stated that 'to activate the Organisation's potential for preventing war, it is necessary from the very beginning to be open about the need for discussion of the situations it is foreseen might break out. A prior requirement for this objective is timely, accurate and unbiased information.'

The previous year, on 5 December 1988, the United Nations General Assembly had already approved a declaration on the prevention and elimination of controversies and situations that could threaten international peace and security and on the role of the United Nations in this sphere (Resolution 43/51). It stated that 'the Security Council ought to consider the possibility of sending, as soon as possible, fact-finding or good offices missions, or of establishing appropriate forms of United Nations presence, including sending observers and peace-keeping operations, a way of preventing subsequent deterioration of the controversy or the situation in the areas under question'.

In the Report for 1990, presented at the height of the Gulf conflict, the demands of the Secretary General were far more explicit, regarding both his own role and the role to be played by the Security Council, considering that:

the peace-making capacity of the United Nations would be considerably strengthened if the Security Council had a peace agenda
that is not confined to items formally inscribed at the request of
the Member States, and if it held periodic meetings to survey the
political scene and identify points of danger at which preventive
or anticipatory diplomacy is required ... Other ways to strengthen
the Council's role in dealing with incipient disputes lie in improving
fact-finding arrangements, in establishing a United Nations presence
in unstable areas and in instituting subsidiary bodies, where appropriate, for preventive diplomacy ... In this context, it needs to be
stressed again that the means at present at the disposal of the
Secretary General for gathering the timely, accurate and unbiased
information that is necessary for averting violent conflicts are
inadequate ... The strategy of peace must reflect a better regard for
timing than has been the case so far. The Organisation's mediatory
or investigative capacity should not be kept in reserve until it is
too late to avert hostilities.[19]

At the end of 1991, the United Nations General Assembly passed
a resolution on the policy of 'fact-finding',[20] which it defines as
'any activity directed at a detailed knowledge of the relevant facts
of any dispute or situation which the competent United Nations bodies
need to efficiently carry out their work in international peace-keeping
and security'. Although it specifies that 'fact-finding must be
exhaustive, unbiased and timely' (paragraph 3), it also states that 'to
send a United Nations fact-finding mission to any state's territory
requires the previous consent of the state involved' (paragraph 6),
which makes it rather unlikely that the information obtained will
be 'exhaustive'. According to this Resolution, states must only 'try'
to admit United Nations missions to their territory (paragraph 21),
leaving it open to them whether they accept or reject the missions.
    These limitations to the practices and the rules of preventive
diplomacy demonstrate the United Nations' need for greater freedom
of movement to carry out impartial investigations into the events
surrounding conflicts, with the object of preventing and resolving
certain national and international conflicts by peaceful means.[21]
Although these fact-finding missions are already used sometimes by
the Secretary General,[22] with mediating and conciliatory measures,
this type of preventive action should be stepped up and a rule made
that acceptance of these missions must be obligatory. This sort of
United Nations judicial police would have to act with complete
freedom anywhere on the planet, at any moment, and without
anyone being able to stop them.[23]

A document by the Palme Commission[24] on the subject of disarmament and security also insisted on this aspect in recommending:

> the use of fact-finding missions and teams of military observers to avoid conflicts arising. It would be of the utmost help if the permanent members of the Security Council agreed to consider the sending of special representatives, observers or fact-finders by the Secretary General as a question not submitted to veto.

However, the United Nations is not a mechanism foreign or alien to the wishes of Member States, but an organ which actually depends on the sum of all their wishes, even if some carry more weight than others. Hence the importance of establishing agreements, treaties and conventions providing a frame of reference so that the activities of the Secretary General can stand up to geopolitical pressures, especially those of the permanent members of the Security Council.

In 1987, the United Nations Office of Research and Collection of Information (ORCI) was set up as a measure of conflict prevention. Its job is to weigh up global trends, prepare outline information on issues and countries or regions, provide early warning of developments in conflict situations, keep up an efficient data base, observe factors relating to possible refugee movements and similar emergency situations, carry out special research and assessment tasks and receive and distribute political information from the media.

Five years after its creation, the ORCI was wound up as a cost-cutting measure and its functions transferred to the two Undersecretary Generals of the Department of Political Affairs. Later, the US has donated an intelligence-processing system to enable the Secretariat better to receive, process and disseminate information.

Whatever formula is chosen (reviving the ORCI, creation of a surveillance agency, verification or control by satellite, etc.), the important thing is that the United Nations should have at its disposal an effective mechanism for the prevention and resolution of conflicts of all types – and not just military conflicts – operating 24 hours a day and working in collaboration with NGOs all over the world, and empowered to take charge of missions such as the following:[25]

- early warning;
- assistance to peace missions;
- providing peace-keeping experts;
- collaboration in solving conflicts of all types;

- training experts in conflict solving, verification and arms negotiations;
- exchanging information on arms and arms control;
- promoting transparency in arms dealing; and
- putting into operation concepts of shared security.

The appointment of Boutros Boutros-Ghali as United Nations Secretary General has given an even greater boost to the doctrine of conflict prevention. In his *Agenda for Peace*,[26] Boutros Boutros-Ghali points out that the United Nations' principal objective is in fact that of preventive diplomacy, which along with peace-making, peace-keeping and peace-building provide the four great pillars of the Organisation's work on peace.

The new Secretary General's preventive programme consists of a range of measures, many of them traditional, directed at avoiding disputes arising between two or more parties and avoiding conflicts, if they arise, from spreading. Analysing and understanding global trends, relieving tensions and containing or controlling conflicts are therefore the purpose of preventive diplomacy.

Confidence-building measures (CBMs) form an initial block, which includes activities such as the exchange of military missions, risk reduction, free movement of information and verification of arms agreements.

Fact-finding by specially appointed officers or teams form the second group of measures, aimed at obtaining a better, more balanced knowledge of the facts, as well as an accurate analysis of global events and trends, be they economic, social, political or military.[27]

Early warning is the third function described and refers to a wide range of problems: threats to the environment, the risk of nuclear accidents, natural disasters, mass population movements, generalised famine threats, the spread of disease, etc., as examples of the non-military dimension of security.

The fourth aspect of this diplomacy is what Boutros Boutros-Ghali calls preventive deployment or, more simply, sending peace-keeping forces in three types of situation: in case of national crisis, at the request of the government or of the parties involved, or with their consent, to carry out humanitarian work, contribute to reconciliation or to enforce security; in differences between states, when two countries consider that a United Nations presence on either side of the border would reduce the risk of hostilities; when a country feels threatened.

One form of preventive deployment contemplated by the Secretary General is that of demilitarised zones situated on either side of a border, with the consent of both parties, so as to separate the contenders, or on one side of the border, to remove all pretext for an attack.

As we can see, information always plays a central role. The Secretary General makes this clear in his Report for 1992, when he says, 'Preventing violations before they occur is of primary importance. The United Nations must be able to identify situations which could degenerate into violations and to take preventive measures' (paragraph 102), or again, 'the United Nations has a crucial responsibility to monitor economic and social trends that may become sources of political tensions, violence and repression' (paragraph 168).

Although Boutros Boutros-Ghali places them under the separate heading of peace-making, the measures aimed at resolving conflicts can also be considered part of a policy of prevention. They include mediation, negotiation, good offices and recourse to the International Court of Justice.

On this last point, it is striking how rarely this organ is used; in the 40 years it has been in existence it has only dealt with 60 cases.[28] Many states still do not accept the Court's jurisdiction as binding, with the result that its rulings are often no more than symbolic. Furthermore, of the five permanent members of the Security Council, four do not accept its rulings as binding,[29] without forgetting that legislative action on human rights by these five states is anything but frequent.[30]

In the difficult process of constructing a system of world governance based on the principles of the Charter and the existence of an effective judicial power in the international sphere, it is evident that in future the International Court of Justice will have to have a far more prominent role than it has to date. But for this to happen it is necessary for all states to accept the Court's authority without reserve, as laid out in Article 36 of its Statute, and for sanctions to be introduced when its rulings are disregarded. Boutros Boutros-Ghali has asked for this to be made a reality before the year 2000, coinciding with the end of the United Nations Decennium for International Law. He has also asked states to contribute to a Trustee Fund set up to provide support for countries who cannot afford the cost involved in submitting their differences to the Court. The countries of Europe have an important role to play here, providing financial resources and technical assistance for any country wanting to present and prepare cases before the Court.

At the moment, the International Court of Justice is a rather baroque institution, cast in the statist mould dominating inter-national law.[31] If it is to undertake new functions it must extend its jurisdiction to individuals, allow access to NGOs concerned with human rights and enlarge the criteria for responsibility, so that it can judge rulers and politicians accused of war crimes. The sentences ought also to consider sanctions.

The Court could also pass judgment on conflicts in which military intervention by the United Nations is requested. In this way, deployment of a military force by the United Nations would be followed by compulsory mediation by the Organisation or by a verdict by the International Court of Justice.[32]

The early warning centres and the rest of the United Nations' activity, however, come up against the principle of non-interference in the internal affairs of states. Although on one hand this principle is a relative guarantee that the militarily more powerful states will not be allowed to systematically interfere in the lives of other weaker states, it is also the case that until now it has not prevented intervention by the powerful to continue, either by arms or by other non-military forms of domination such as the money market, trade or transnational business.

The principle of non-intervention, however, is an old taboo which grants immunity to those who systematically violate human rights. This old dogma therefore needs revising, and it would be a good thing if this took place in the context of the reform and democratisation of the United Nations so as to decide whether this organisation has the juridical and material capacity, apart from the moral legitimacy, to intervene in certain affairs of states in extreme cases of injustice.

United Nations Resolution 688 (1991) condemning Iraq's repression of the Kurds and allowing humanitarian organisations access to the towns affected, while not authorising the use of force, established a precedent for the acceptance of a certain right of intervention. In the short term, the first step in this process towards intervention could probably be based on the principle that no state may prevent humanitarian aid being sent or received[33] and that the defence of human rights ranks higher than national sovereignty. The growing involvement of the peace-keeping forces in humanitarian operations and the pitiful conditions of security in which some supplies have had to be distributed (the cases of Somalia and former Yugoslavia, for example) could help to set the basis for a new doctrine of humanitarian intervention which, however necessary it may be, and in view of the traditional discrimination by the Security Council and its double standard of values,[34] will not be free of conflictive interpretations or straightforwardly negative ones (for example, the case of Somalia in the second half of 1993).

Obviously, and however difficult this may be, any preventive policy that hopes to get to the root of a problem must pay greater attention to tensions and conflicts arising from economic and social inequalities, in both their internal and external dimensions. However surprising and insincere it might seem, the Security Council itself actually recognised, at its summit meeting of 31 January 1992, that 'peace and prosperity are inseparable, and that lasting peace and stability call for effective international co-operation to eliminate poverty and promote a better life for everyone, within a broader concept of freedom',[35] and that 'the non-military causes of instability in the economic, social, humanitarian and ecological spheres have become a threat to peace and security, for which reason all the countries belonging to the United Nations must give maximum priority to solving these questions'.

But peace, stability and conflict prevention are not achieved with fine words, so much as through political and social commitments to transform the present situation, characterised as it is by the large number of the planet's inhabitants whose basic needs are not satisfied. This fact must necessarily lead to a profound change in the attitudes of the privileged dominant countries. The differences between rich and poor and the degradation of the environment are in this sense the most serious problems facing the international community. As Urquhart and Childers point out,[36] these problems 'can only be prevented through better and more sustainable development, which among other things will call for effective population planning, improvements in primary health services, more technical education and training, modifications to agricultural policies, renewable energy sources, external aid and trade and financial agreements that are more stable, more predictable and more favourable to the developing countries'. In short, a calendar of courageous, specific measures, not of empty words and stinginess.

Conflict prevention is the only existing alternative for successfully solving today's problems. Maurice Bertrand is right[37] when he says that taken to its ultimate consequences this policy of prevention represents a genuine intellectual and moral revolution. His suggestion that $200,000 or $300,000 million be assigned to this purpose each year through 'regional Marshall plans' for countries with identifiable risks is far more sensible than turning a blind eye to the problem as we are doing today. The basic outlines of these plans, like providing new social projects for peoples without hope, organising strict control on arms deals or extending the OSCE's confidence measures across the globe, also coincide with the ideas laid out here.

Future conditions of life on our planet – in other words, the safety of the future – depends on our ability to answer this challenge and come up with a solution. As it is no longer possible to defer solutions for future generations, the response to the challenge of change must be found in a responsible complicity of people and institutions today. The United Nations could play a central role in this alliance, though not alone, so long as it carries out its overdue democratising reform.

The question, in short, is that the United Nations should not only operate reactively – that is, through crisis diplomacy – but through an essentially preventive diplomacy before conflicts break out. As has been pointed out by a former United Nations official with a considerable knowledge of the organisation, the question we need to ask is whether or not this is the right moment for the United Nations to create, finance and maintain a system based on surveillance, consensus, collective action and international law – in other words, to return to the very premises of the United Nations Charter.[38]

Proposals

- Create the necessary mechanisms within the United Nations and the regional organisations for detecting and predicting conflicts.
- Revive the United Nations ORCI or an agency to carry out its functions.
- Prevention should be directed not only at military questions, but also at political, economic, ecological, social, cultural and technological problems.
- Special attention should be paid to ethnic and ecological conflicts.
- Early warning should take place simultaneously at different levels (national, regional and international) and through different institutions (governmental and non-governmental).
- Create a global communications network linking all the early warning centres, whether governmental, NGO or belonging to international organisations, using the same computer language.
- Decentralising the United Nations would make it possible to establish early warning centres in all the associated regional organisations.
- Develop regional mechanisms for mediation.
- Potentiate the OSCE's Conflict Prevention Centre.
- Ensure mechanisms for immediate response to emergency situations (advance commitment).
- Connect early warning centres to arms control and verification organs.

- Set up a disarmament verification agency within the United Nations, with the appropriate technical means, including those obtained by satellite.
- Establish a Convention by which some military satellites are transferred to new missions and come under the control of the United Nations.
- Increase the powers of the United Nations Secretary General to investigate conflictive situations, either directly or by means of fact-finding missions and observers.
- Increase the presence of the United Nations in unstable areas, including the peace-keeping forces.
- Establish the rule that United Nations fact-finding missions must be accepted, that they can take place anywhere, at any moment and under any circumstances, and that they cannot be vetoed by the five permanent members of the Security Council.
- Improve relations between the United Nations and the NGOs carrying out monitoring and conflict prevention tasks.
- Foment the training of specialists in conflict prevention and regulation and disarmament verification.
- Develop military and non-military confidence-building measures (CBM).
- Make all states accept the authority of the International Court of Justice without reserve and apply sanctions when its rulings are disregarded.
- Contribute to the Court's Trust Fund to provide assistance for countries that cannot afford the legal costs and do not have the necessary preparation for attending the Court.
- Tie certain interventionist operations by the United Nations to the Court's rulings.
- Extend the Court's jurisdiction to individuals, make it accessible to NGOs concerned with human rights and enlarge the criterion of responsibility for judging governments accused of war crimes.
- Revise the principle of non-intervention in cases of severe violations of human rights, urgent humanitarian aid or natural or ecological catastrophes.
- Accept the principle that no state can prevent humanitarian aid being sent or received.
- Pay greater attention to tensions and conflicts arising from economic and social inequalities.

4

Humanitarian Intervention

The events of recent years forced us to meditate on our position regarding the tragedies abroad which discomfort us and question the human condition itself. Somalia, Yugoslavia and Rwanda have at least provoked debate as to the limits we impose on humanitarian action, on our inability to regulate conflicts and our attitude to other people's suffering. Despite repeated appeals, the United Nations has also been unable to come up with a satisfactory answer to either of these two conflicts. Collective response has failed resoundingly.

Not long ago, the operation to help the Kurds led to discussion on the opportuneness or legitimacy of so-called 'humanitarian intervention'; that is, military intervention motivated by humanitarian considerations. Sometimes, not always, starving or sick refugees have become the object of attention of a discomfited, horrified public, who stare helplessly at scenes on television of enormous cruelty, scenes that create a feeling of guilt and a generalised uneasiness that opens the doors to attitudes in favour of military intervention as a means of solving or mitigating these situations.

The question raised by humanitarian intervention, understood as multilateral armed intervention against another state without the consent of its government, is how to reconcile the principles of the territorial sovereignty of states, non-interference in their internal affairs and the prohibition of the use of force, stipulated in the United Nations Charter, with the defence of human rights in extreme situations, when their violation represents a threat to international security and peace.[1]

Humanitarian intervention raises doubts, misgivings and fears, even in those who support it with a certain conviction. This is because on a political level, even if there is confusion over the meaning of what is humanitarian, we are perfectly aware of the perversions of traditional interventionism.

The United Nations and its blue helmets play a central role in this issue, if we take it that only through this international organisation can we bestow legitimacy on a new doctrine and perhaps a new force specialised in this type of mission. The risk of a mistaken analysis or of mistaken proposals and the confusion created over the varieties of humanitarian intervention already existing should not frighten

52

us or deter us from the necessary work of clarifying the good and bad points in these ideas.

In view of what has happened in some recent operations, the suspicion exists that the United Nations is a cover for power-seeking on the part of old and new powers who want to establish forms of influence in areas not allocated during the Cold War, and that its instrumentalisation in recent conflicts, especially during the Gulf War, has started a trend towards the privatisation of some of its functions, which are coming under the control of the United States or, in some cases, of NATO as a kind of armed wing of the United Nations.[2]

Alain Joxe suggested a very simple but clarifying way of approaching this thorny topic.[3] In his opinion, there are two clearly discernible types of United Nations expedition, distinguishable by the colour of the helmet and the armed vehicles, which symbolise two kinds of mandate:

- United Nations expeditions supported by the United States (Lebanon, Cambodia, Yugoslavia, Somalia-I, etc.), with blue helmets and white vehicles. He calls this type of United Nations expedition 'garrison' expeditions (type A).
- United States expeditions supported by the United Nations (Persian Gulf, Somalia-II), with war helmets and camouflaged vehicles. These are 'expeditionary' missions (type B).

For Joxe, and this is an opinion shared by many other people, the participation of the United States in operations under its mandate (type B) must always have a low human cost and be of short duration. They use the United Nations umbrella as a simple complement to the internal juridical mechanism, since these expeditions are in fact no more than a unilateral move by the United States, decided by Congress and supported afterwards by an 'ad hoc' international coalition.

The 'garrison' expeditions (type A), on the other hand, tend to be long, or at times permanent. Hence the term 'garrison', which refers to the concept of policing or fixed presence in an area of tension.

Having made this initial clarification, Joxe accepts the traditional classification, also used by the United Nations Secretary General, which distinguished between peace-keeping operations, humanitarian operations and military operations. The first of these is the typical operation involving blue helmets or blue berets, and which we shall analyse later in greater detail. The third implies acceptance of the use of force on a multinational basis, and will also be treated in another chapter. On the other hand, the second takes us onto more shaky ground, since humanitarian aid operations may or may not be accompanied by the use of force. What do those people who devote themselves to the work of humanitarian aid have to say about this possibility?

Populations in Danger is the title of a magnificent book written and published by a Médecins Sans Frontières team[4] and centring on a description of the ten most serious cases of populations in danger of disappearing: former Yugoslavia, the Tuaregs, Mozambique, Somalia, Sudan, Iraq, Nagorno Karabakh, Sri Lanka, Myanmar and Peru. Ten cases characterised essentially by internal conflicts or violence, population movements caused by these political crises and in some cases by famine or epidemics, always in a context of extreme tension.

In the words of the president of the International Council of MSF, the book is 'an appeal to the mobilisation of intelligence and the wish to understand, as well as solidarity and the capacity for indignation and action'. And it is in this spirit that under the significant heading 'What there is at stake', seven members of MSF claim that the 'humanitarian tactic' of states is an old trick, an alibi to offset their lack of political action and calm the guilty conscience of peaceful citizens, because humanitarian action, when not carried out in a context of profound transformation of global economic relations, is no more than a mask for neglect and indignity.

The condemnation, made with profound disappointment, comes from people who offer their time, their energy, their skills and their humanity in situations of the most extreme hardship. Bosnia and Somalia are in this respect the two most obvious examples of the way in which humanitarian organisations, used as aspirins to numb people's awareness, have become bogged down, at the same time as they are often the only effective formula for relieving the suffering of thousands of human beings. This is their complaint, but also their greatness.

In the words of one contributor, 'the rich nations once again accept the hardship of peoples as an inevitable fate, a result of the "criminalization" of their political context'. If some kind of official aid is nevertheless sent, it is administered as a simple recourse of foreign policy, like a way of exerting influence, at the same time as it takes their mind off their inability to act to contain or avoid the situations that cause these tragedies.

With their individual commitment to refugees, these associations show their disappointment at the lack of political action in the face of ethnic cleansing and the control of territories through forced displacement of populations. Referring to the conflict in Yugoslavia, they do not hesitate to point out that the international community, having failed to face up to its political responsibilities from the start of the conflict, has had no option but to accompany this hateful process with humanitarian aid, although it declines its obligations on the grounds of not wanting to facilitate 'ethnic cleansing' and that 'humanitarian aid has merely played an accompanying or even auxiliary role in a strategy of territorial conquest and ethnic cleansing'.

It is interesting in this respect that sources in the European Commission itself have recognised that if the Twelve have allowed community spending on humanitarian aid to take off ($872 million for Yugoslavia between September 1991 and June 1993) it has been precisely to satisfy their guilty consciences and make up for the lack of political or even military solutions, because from the financial point of view – and the same sources – an all-out military operation would in fact have been cheaper.[5]

Sadako Ogata, United Nations High Commissioner for Refugees, also spoke out against the (de)politicisation of humanitarianism, at the International Conference for the protection of war victims (Geneva, 31 August 1993), when she said that:

> humanitarian efforts must not contribute to delaying or even replacing political negotiation. On the other hand, they must not be used as a means of achieving military or political objectives. Nevertheless, humanitarian institutions are manipulated and blackmailed more and more, and the aid they supply is taken advantage of by the conflicting parties as a means to their own non-humanitarian ends.

In this tone of sincerity and honesty, another contributor to the MSF book states that:

> never had humanitarian action been so much in demand. Politicians look on it more and more as an especially adequate response to conflict situations. However, we nevertheless find that the humanitarian argument has never been so difficult and, in many cases, so disappointing as in the new conflicts arising today.

MSF's message to the United Nations is clear: it must redefine the mandate given its agencies and its forces so as to provide them with effective means of halting a war, instead of making them keep a tally of the number of cease-fires that are not respected, and give the humanitarian agencies greater autonomy so that the logic of political domination and the logic of co-ordinating human aid do not parasitise each other mutually, as in the cases of Somalia, Bosnia and, especially, Iraq.

Humanitarian intervention in its non-military dimension is necessary for the survival of millions of people, but in its present form it is also a drug that disguises the real nature of the illness. Joxe[6] rightly speaks of the 'humanitarianisation of problems'; that is, a sweetened way of dealing with questions, which prevents responsibilities being assumed when barbarism is unleashed (those of Europe in Yugoslavia or those of the United States in Somalia, for example). For Joxe, 'the choice of Somalia, instead of Mozambique, in which to put into practice this humanitarian interventionism, seems to be a publicity choice rather than a political one, because it brings the humanitarian element to the fore'. There is no reason why anyone should still remember the arms sales to this poor country, or the use of its territory in the nuclear strategy of the Cold War, and there is no reason why anyone should suspect that the deployment in Somalia could be seen as a 'precautionary measure in the framework of the protection of the Gulf', or a warning to Iran as to the limits to the influence allowed it. With the humanitarianisation of conflicts, there are only victims, never culprits. Criticism of past and present and the analysis of options for the future become unnecessary, because the magnanimous empire provides relief, with the help of the United Nations, wherever it is needed.

But what happens is that very often the relief arrives in the wrong conditions and too late. In Somalia, for example, the United Nations agencies and some NGOs failed to react in time to the first warnings of food shortages in 1987. The results of this lack of foresight were catastrophic.[7] Five years later, this time surrounded by television publicity, food relief was excessive and therefore harmful, to the extent that local agricultural prices plummeted and there was no incentive to gather crops.[8]

'Humanitarianism', when it is badly organised and stems from the guilty conscience of wealthy countries, can also cause hardship. If it is also accompanied or followed by an offensive military intervention, failure is assured.

In spite of all this instrumentalisation, there is no getting away from the fact that humanitarian aid is necessary. But under what conditions can it not have this sedative and exculpatory effect which humanitarian agencies themselves are so quick to criticise? Perhaps by analysing the problems it presents we could come up with some answers.

Chemillier-Gendreau and Salamé[9] point to three great contradictions of humanitarian interventions, from which a few principles can be deduced:

- After the storm (and the relief), situations arising from underlying causes of a structural nature surface again in all their horror. There is no definitive solution, therefore, until one gets to the root of the evil.
- Humanitarian intervention is selective, not only as regards the countries in which intervention takes place, but also in the time that interest lasts. Its great defect is that it confuses sedation with cure, a short-lived effect with a lasting situation, when not in itself counterproductive. Intervention of this sort must be universal, and always respond to a previously established type of situation, whatever its origin, and must be accompanied by back-up action to impose real respect for the rule of law.
- It is wrong to believe that intervention can operate in two stages, with an initial strike by the United States (televised humanitarianism) followed by a long-term United Nations intervention (Joxe's 'garrison' intervention). Humanitarian actions must be administered collectively, from beginning to end. The action must be assured by responsible commitment on the part of the whole of the reformed United Nations, and not by the initial predisposition of the White House. In this respect, the case of Somalia is clarifying, as well as pathetic.

Unless we have a clearer idea of what we are after, unless we ensure that these activities have no connection with imperial or colonial intervention, we cannot possibly understand any proposed form of humanitarian intervention. Salamé[10] leaves us in no doubt:

humanitarianism here, legalism there, strategy over there. The West explains the reasons for its military expeditions to its own satisfaction. It doesn't explain them to the South, which far from being content to see how the same soldiers invade them more and more often and each time with a different argument, each time exhibiting new motivations drawn from television audiences rather than from the beneficent objectives of the operation.

The fact is, of course, that history has not changed to the extent that we can trust those who for decades or centuries have raised the flag of freedom, religion or democracy in defence of their own interests and privileges. Strategy, interference and humanitarian policy, something very different from a solidary and humanitarian conscience, is in this sense a kind of minimalist morality, a value beneath which we shelter,[11] avoiding political action, which it replaces. As Prunier points out, 'humanitarian action is getting to be like an ideological ritual, in which we are not expected to face up to the complexity of reality, but to replace it so as to ease our conscience'. And it is when we are caught in this trap that we can understand the warnings of Médecins Sans Frontières or the words of the United Nations special envoy for aid to refugees in the war in former Yugoslavia, José María Mendiluce, when he admits that:

> as I personally see it, passive humanitarianism is over. We have decided on humanitarian agitation, stirring the consciences of the self-satisfied population ... We must pass the message on; tell them that even if they don't care about children in Bosnia, they ought to care about their own children; because if this war goes on, if all the fanatics and hate-mongers go on winning here, some day they will eventually contaminate all of us.[12]

In extreme cases like those of Bosnia, Somalia and others, humanitarian intervention is an obligation, and military intervention a possibility to be considered. But unless it has been preceded by all the humanitarian efforts possible, unless we have been capable of stirring our conscience and our comfort and unless we have previously established mechanisms for conflict prevention and disarmament, military intervention will be no more than a limited and unsuccessful substitute for political and social activity, or in other words, for our obligation to involve ourselves in finding solutions to conflictive processes by attacking the problem at the roots.

Humanitarian interventionism, in its present form, doesn't work and is ambiguous and opportunistic, because the general principles behind these operations do little to hide the interests – or indifference – of states. But a form must be found in which it can be carried out in the future legitimately and coherently. According to Médecins Sans Frontières,[13] intervention in the last few years has in truth responded to calculated home and foreign policy interests, as well as the concerns of competing developed countries anxious to make their presence felt in the humanitarian and military terrain and of their need to demonstrate with elegance the usefulness of their armed forces following the disappearance of the capital risk of an East–West confrontation, as a result of which the military have become the spearhead of the universal philanthropy.

But there will be no legitimate interventions until a framework for international procedure in extreme crisis situations has been discussed, agreed and accepted. Until this agreement is reached, foreign intervention can add a new dimension to the problem, rather than provide a long-term solution. For the time being, international mobilisation is still selective and responds to political interests, media impact and the pressure of public opinion. Everything therefore points to a new geography of international intervention, ranging from intervention in forgotten tragedies (Sudan) to military interventions classed as humanitarian (Somalia), and including intervention by regional organisations of powers (Liberia) and peace-making operations in conflicts arising in the wake of the Cold War (Cambodia).

What is in question is a society in which compassion, another name for solidarity, tends to be replaced with a decaffeinated version that ignores the demands of justice; in which information, often manipulated, is artfully elbowed out by communication, politics and rhetoric, truth by image and knowledge by emotion. What can be done in this situation? According to MSF, if the relief organisations are not to become partners in this game of manipulations, they must react by fulfilling their essential duties, that is to continue to make use of the means accompanying these mobilisations (in response to the immediate needs of the victims), reflect on their work, demonstrating that their action is backed up by more solid principles than the short-lived emotions they feel tempted to negotiate with and, as they point out in *Populations in Danger*, denouncing the fact that when there are victims there are also culprits, in other words, that there are also responsibilities to be faced when savagery is unleashed.

In short, humanitarian intervention must not disguise the true nature of the problem, otherwise it just perpetuates it. The NGOs acting in this field have an enormous responsibility here. If they are critical and independent, and avoid the trap of what is known as 'philanthropic imperialism' – self-satisfied uncritical attitudes in the face of political scandals – then as well as fulfilling the tasks entrusted to them they can also act as genuine alert centres for the prevention of conflict situations. To achieve this, though, some of them will have to revise their traditional fundraising methods, rejecting communicative impact strategies based on the 'pornography of hunger', instead promoting campaigns for political and social awareness which will allow more lasting solutions to get under way.

In countries where there are United Nations peace operations, the NGOs can also monitor the activities of the international organisations. The communiqués by some NGOs operating in Somalia, for example, in which they denounced the militarisation of UNOSOM, the bureaucracy of the United Nations, the escalation of violence against the civilian population, the insufficient activity of the United Nations in the reconciliation process and the violations of human rights during certain military operations, all go to show that it is possible to carry out humanitarian work without falling prey to ingenuity.

Protecting Refugees

Drought and war are the cause each year of an exodus of millions of people. According to the United Nations High Commission for Refugees (UNHCR), there are some 23 million refugees in the world, as well as another 26 million displaced people within their own countries as a result of civil war, famine or natural disasters. This means that one out of every 15 people in the world has been forced to flee from home.

What is more, large-scale emigration is no longer a thing of the Third World alone. With the war in former Yugoslavia, Europe has recently experienced one of the military episodes which has generated the largest number of internal displacements and refugees. Three and a half million people from the different republics of the former Yugoslav Federation have swelled the ranks of the refugees or the displaced people, and large waves of refugees from the countries of the East are expected in Europe in the next few years.

The figures for refugees often reach horrifying proportions. Five million people fled as a result of the war in Afghanistan, almost a third of the population, of whom three million took refuge in Pakistan and two million in Iran. War and poverty have forced one million people out of Somalia, one of the poorest countries in the world, towards countries which are equally affected by famine such as Ethiopia and Kenya. There are also approximately one million refugees from Mozambique in other southern African countries.

In the countries receiving them, the arrival of large numbers of refugees has a severe impact. Guinea-Conakry has to sustain a volume of refugees (more than half a million) equal to 10 per cent of its population; in Burundi and Malawi, the proportion is similar. There are three million Afghans in Pakistan. Before repatriation, there were 350,000 Cambodians in Thailand, 270,000 Burmese in Bangladesh, 200,000 Angolans in Zaire, 700,000 Ethiopians in the Sudan. As we can see, it is always the neighbouring countries, which are just as poor, that have to take in all these thousands of people fleeing from their own homes, normally on foot, in search of somewhere where survival is guaranteed.

The proximity of Yugoslavia and Europe's inability to act quickly in response to the appeals for humanitarian assistance that form part of these displacements has demonstrated the lack of insight and the irresponsibility of those who have the means to relieve the suffering of refugees, an issue which until recently was considered remote, a Third World problem subject to the laws of compassion and goodwill governing contributions by well-off countries. No credit was given to the possible participation of the industrialised countries in the background causes of these mass displacements and therefore their moral obligation to take part in the reconstruction of the countries affected, help in the repatriation of refugees, see that the return of these people was organised according to humanitarian principles and avoid the obligatory return of populations until their security was guaranteed.

Afghanistan is a case in point. More than ten years of warfare produced one million dead, two million wounded and five million refugees. In June 1992, the United Nations Secretary General made an urgent appeal for $180 million in aid, almost 53 of which were for the repatriation of 200,000 Afghans. Response to the international communiqué has been very limited, as it is now a question of rebuilding a shattered country and not of fighting an essentially useful enemy. Nevertheless, in the five year period 1987–91, many countries sold heavy weaponry to Afghanistan for a total value of $8,430 million. Most of this came from the Soviet Union ($8,125 million) and the rest from the United States ($149 million), China ($48 million) and the United Kingdom ($43 million), amongst other suppliers.[14] There was no difficulty in exporting arms to Afghanistan, but gathering 2 per cent of the value of these arms for humanitarian aid posed a problem. The same goes for many other cases, from Somalia or Ethiopia to Iraq, in which displacement has been preceded by wars fired by a lively trade in arms. Those who have contributed most to destroying a country should commit themselves most during the reconstruction phase.

El Salvador is another clear example of the limited effect and profitability of 'military solutions'. During the 1980s, the government of El Salvador spent $2,500 million, thanks to generous North-American military aid, in a failed attempt to put an end to the war with the FMLN guerrillas. This strategy left 80,000 dead and the country in ruins. Subsequently, during 1990 and 1991, the United Nations were able to put into effect the peace process with only $70 million. Investing in reconciliation is, needless to say, more profitable and more beneficial in human as well as economic terms.

The arms trade is an intrinsically perverse activity, for the seller and for the buyer, as it stimulates the delusion that accumulating destructive artefacts will dissuade a hypothetical adversary. History is filled with examples of the opposite result – that is, purchases of large quantities of weapons feeding conflicts and making them more deadly. It is therefore surprising that although its final results are known there is so little interest in reducing it.

The cost of the peace-keeping operations begun in 1991 came to almost $4,000 million by 1993. This is the price the international community will have to pay to douse the fires that the permanent members of the Security Council themselves helped to kindle with their sales of arms. According to figures from the ACDA,[15] in the five-year period 1985–9, arms to a value of more than $34,000 million were sold to the following countries in which United Nations forces are at present intervening: Iraq, Kuwait, Angola, former Yugoslavia, Mozambique, Morocco, El Salvador and Somalia. Seventy-seven per cent of these arms exports came from the five permanent members of the Security Council. The answer to this paradox is obvious and can be summed up in the old saying 'You shall reap what you shall sow' – or, amounting to the same thing, if you don't want to have to send peace-making forces to a country some day, don't sell it weapons in the first place.

The case of Yugoslavia, while not unique, has also shown the difficulty of distributing the relief obtained, especially food, and the limitations to the freedom of movement of the international organisations supplying this aid, very often at a risk to their own lives.

Relief mechanisms must therefore be urgently improved and amplified, and at the same time proper distribution of aid must be ensured by a suitable protection force. As Médecins Sans Frontières has requested, freedom of assessment and right to control the movement of aid should form the inviolable basis for any forthcoming rules of humanitarian assistance. After all, the aim is to avoid relief food supplies from becoming a devastating weapon in the hands of political powers, a new means of oppression.[16] The United Nations peace forces have an urgent and unmistakable calling, and they ought to have permanent units at their disposal, trained and prepared for this specific role. The traumatic experience in Somalia, further-more, shows that this protection or distribution force must not be confused with traditional military forces, since the two jobs do not seem to be compatible. In the final instance the recipient of aid must come to see the 'blue helmet' as a co-operating friend, not as an invader, and vice versa, the 'blue helmet' must not look on the recipient of aid as a possible enemy or adversary. Only under these general conditions is there any sense in sending a force specialised in distributing humanitarian aid.

The economic problem is the first thing we must look at. In 1994, the UNHCR had a budget of $1,200 million for dealing with the tragedy of refugees – in other words, an average of $52 per refugee. This sum is obviously much lower than the average amount corresponding to each soldier there is in the world ($32,800). To put it another way, for every dollar the world spends on a refugee, it spends $630 on military ends.

Table 4.1 Comparison between military expenditure and attention to refugees

World military expenditure	$920,000 million
Number of soldiers	28 million
Expenditure per soldier	$32,800
UNHCR budget for 1994	$1,200 million
Number of refugees	23 million
Expenditure per refugee	$52

This disparity between military funds and humanitarian aid, although universal, does not do justice to the attention afforded to refugees by certain countries. Contributions to UNHCR programmes in the first eight months of 1994 reached $609 million, of which more than 20 per cent came from three Nordic countries: Sweden, Norway and Denmark. The contribution by these three countries to the UNHCR is 60 times the global average in this period. There is also a noticeable correlation between the countries that contribute most to aid for refugees and those that take part most often in the United Nations peace operations.

The budgets and the means for attending to refugees are clearly insufficient, even supposing that the contributions requested by the UNHCR were promptly paid up. It is therefore worth looking to see what material means could be made available to the UNHCR and other international organisations so that they could accomplish their objectives satisfactorily, what part of these could come from present military potential and what role the peace forces could play in refugee aid.

As the United Nations High Commissioner for Refugees, Sadako Ogata, pointed out to the UNHCR Executive Committee:[17]

in the face of emergencies on an unprecedented scale, we have had to turn on occasion to the military for logistical support. It has given a new dimension to humanitarian operations as well as to the role of the military in the post-Cold War era. When peace and compassion replace war and destruction, when the enormous logistical capacity of the military is channelled into non-political, humanitarian purposes, in co-operation with Governments, United Nations agencies and NGOs, I believe we all stand to gain.

In areas where there has been open warfare, this relief comes up against the problem of the mining of a large part of the territory. The United Nations has begun a programme of co-ordinated action to clear mines, in which the Humanitarian Affairs Department, the Department of Peace-keeping Operations and other organs are taking part. In Afghanistan, for example, there are about ten million mines, and almost half a million people have already been crippled as a result. The Office for the co-ordination of humanitarian and economic aid programmes (UNOCA) has 2,000 mine clearers in the area at present, under the auspices of Afghan NGOs. In Cambodia, 1,500 people are working to clear the five million mines scattered over the country. In Mozambique it is calculated that there are some two million mines. A United Nations Peace Force could tackle this important problem, organising multinational groups of sappers to defuse mines. Once again, the countries supplying the mines should take greater care to resolve this aspect, with both military and medical support.

The transfer to humanitarian ends of part of the funds now devoted to military communication also forms part of this approach. Since 1975, the FAO has had a Global Information and Warning System for Food and Agriculture (GIWS), in which 100 countries, several international organisations and more than 50 NGOs take part. Its principal objectives are to keep a permanent watch on the food supply-and-demand situation, identify countries or regions where food shortages are imminent and evaluate the possible need for urgent relief supplies of food. It makes ample use of meteorological data and information supplied by satellite in supervising crop conditions and detecting droughts.

The GIWS provides an example of how information and space communications at the service of humanitarian ends dignify technology and contribute to a policy of prevention. Improving this surveillance network, creating similar networks in other fields and committing states to attend to their demands are some of the challenges outstanding.

One of the proposals of the Second Conference for a More Democratic United Nations (CAMDUN-2) which is directed at reinforcing prevention consists in establishing a rescue programme making use of rapid global response, to provide humanitarian aid within twelve hours in response to any disaster situation. It would make use of existing military resources, which would be passed to a warehouse for rescue supplies and airborne rescue teams, which in turn would co-ordinate the activities of the United Nations (Disaster Office) with the Red Cross and the Red Crescent.

The World Food Programme (WFP) for refugees tries to distribute 15 kilos of wheat a month and 900 grams of edible oil to each refugee. In some cases, the UNHCR distributes food and money for repatriated families, instead of providing daily meals. In Afghanistan, for example, each family receives $135, seeds and 300 kilos of grain, enough to feed it for three or four months while it starts a new life.

Ensuring that these millions of refugees are fed calls for daunting transport and distribution logistics. Hundreds of thousands of tonnes of food have to be transported every month, and not always under the easiest conditions since the country affected is very often in a region also suffering the ravages of drought or war. Rebuilding damaged infrastructures to allow the entrance of relief is another of the jobs to be taken on by any relief operation to refugees and areas affected by drought.

The case of the former Yugoslavia has raised the problem of how to supply humanitarian aid in situations of open warfare. The enormous difficulty of getting food to towns under siege in the interior made it necessary to establish an airlift, which operated equally precariously and intermittently in spite of the considerable logistics.

The UNHCR estimated that 9,226 tonnes a week of food and other supplies would be needed to attend to the 1.6 million inhabitants of Bosnia and Herzegovina during the winter of 1992–3. In the period from July 1992 to March 1993, UNHCR aid to Sarajevo reached the figure of 47,187 tonnes, 60 per cent of which was sent by air and the remaining 40 per cent by land. This means an average of 1,400 tonnes a week. In the same period, the UNHCR has transported 26,100 tonnes to Croatia. The challenge is impressive, both for the UNHCR and for the international community.

Apart from the problem of the lack of security on these flights as a result of the lack of dissuasive power on the part of the United Nations forces 'protecting' these convoys, the magnitude of the figures for refugees or displaced people and for the quantities of food, medicines and other supplies points to the need to organise a stable transport corps available to (or under the control of) the United Nations Peace Forces.

The transport of certain products (perishable goods or medicines), the need for urgency or the impossibility of moving the material any other way call for the use of heavy transport aircraft. The air forces of the countries of the OSCE have more than 1,800 aircraft of this type, capable of transporting in one journey more than 68,000 metric tons. Why not put this immense military transport capacity at the service of humanitarian aid?

The simple exercise of comparing the OSCE's fleet of heavy transport aircraft with the flights made during a few months of the Sarajevo airlift (July–September 1992) gives us an idea of what could be done and of the differences in disposition between one country and another. Denmark, France, Canada and Sweden were in this sense the most generous in proportion to their transport capacity, while Russia and the United States were the most frugal.

The four countries that contributed most aircraft mobilised the equivalent of one of their heavy transport military aircraft every 17 days. The Danish average, the largest, was of one aircraft every 3.3 days, while Spain's was one aircraft every 75 days.

Table 4.2 Sarajevo airlift (3 July to 3 September 1992)

	No. flights	*(*)*
France	182	3.5
Germany	173	2.0
United States	170	0.2
Italy	140	2.8
United Kingdom	122	2.6
Canada	100	3.1
Belgium	28	2.3
Sweden	27	3.4
Turkey	21	0.8
Denmark	18	6.0
Others	43	
TOTAL	1,024	0.6
tonnes	12,405	

(*) Number of flights over the country's total number of heavy transport military aircraft.

A guideline for the future could involve each country's airforce making a significant part of their heavy transport aircraft permanently available to the United Nations, which would give the Organisation considerable manoeuvring capacity, with about 600 aircraft available to it for its relief work if each country lent it a third of its aircraft.

Table 4.3 Heavy transport aircraft that could be made available to the United Nations

United States	250
Russia	150
Rest of Europe	200
Others	50
TOTAL	650

The United Nations ought to ensure that a significant number of aircraft are available for use on each continent so as to save work and increase the efficiency of operations. The loan of military bases and installations for use in United Nations operations would facilitate the logistics of this work.[18]

The aircraft made available to the United Nations would preferably be used for operations directed or requested by the Organisation itself. Some missions might also make use of smaller transport craft belonging to countries closer to the theatre of operations. Although they cannot normally carry more than six tonnes, there are a lot of them and they perform excellently in support roles.

In many other cases, food can be transported on boats and trucks. All armies have transport vehicles, with a load capacity of between four and ten tonnes each. These could be made available to the United Nations for humanitarian aid operations, especially for transporting food and carrying refugees.

In 1992, for example, the UNHCR organised 20 operations for repatriating 1.7 million people and providing relief for another 720,000 who it is hoped will return to their country of their own accord. The total cost of the operations was $400 million. According to the UNHCR, sending someone back to their country costs less than twice what it costs to keep them in a camp for a year.

The International Organisation for Migration (IOM) has a transport system which was used by 20 per cent of the Afghans repatriated. Complementing this through the temporary loan of military transport vehicles from countries neighbouring on the centre of operations is another job to be carried out.

Some countries with naval forces have transport craft which could be assigned to United Nations humanitarian missions. The advantage of these boats is their enormous cargo capacity, which can vary between 2,000 and 20,000 tonnes. The transport capacity of these ships was amply demonstrated in the Gulf War, in which the United States mobilised dozens of boats of all sorts. Suffice it to say that the material and equipment carried on advance sea craft during the first fortnight of August would have needed 2,100 flights by gigantic C-5 transport planes.[19] The Reserve Force mobilised 42 boats and another 73 merchant vessels were chartered from private owners. In view of the size of these figures, it seems worth looking at the naval potential that could be made use of in relief operations.

Attention to refugees and food distribution are two of the fundamental tasks the future United Nations Peace Force will have to take on. Both the United Nations and the military staff of many countries already have ample experience in this field, enough to understand current difficulties and shortcomings.[20] The creation of mechanisms within the United Nations to command and control these operations and supervise the training and specialisation of military officers and civilian personnel for these tasks, as well as the implementation of an effective policy of co-operation and co-ordination, are among the challenges the United Nations will have to face in the coming years.

Several countries have, in the last few years, taken part unilaterally or jointly in aid operations. Operation 'Provide Comfort' mobilised 13,000 people and transported 7,000 tonnes of material to help the Kurds; Operation 'Sea Angel' involved 8,000 North-American soldiers and 6,000 tonnes of aid for Bangladesh. Though questionable in many respects, these experiences could be extremely useful in designing a United Nations Peace Force. Sweden and Switzerland, two neutral countries, have already set up special rapid intervention units for humanitarian aid. The US Department of Defense also has a special office which organises logistical support for disaster situations. The Russian Federation, for its part, has also created an operations unit along similar lines.[21]

Obviously, attention to refugees and distribution of food and medicines to people ravaged by war or famine does not remove the various underlying causes of these situations. But the obstacles and the resistance to a radical cure for these ills (corruption, militarism, the aftermath of colonialism,[22] dictatorships, trade relations unfavourable to the South, etc.) must not serve as an excuse to abandon millions of people to certain death. The participation of United Nations forces in this relief work ought to be the start of a commitment by the Security Council and by the whole of the United Nations, aimed at eradicating the problem.

Until action is taken which is directed at the roots of the issue, states should at least commit themselves to improving and strengthening already existing mechanisms, as summed up by Sadako Ogata in these six aspects:

- Reinforce the emergency response.
- Find solutions for the return of refugees.
- Develop preventive measures.
- Strengthen international protection.
- Increase collaboration, both of governments and of international organisations and NGOs.
- Improve the administration of existing resources.

Let me say once more that aid to refugees is no more than an obligation arising from our inability to resolve the underlying causes. Because, as Sadako Ogata says in reference to the Yugoslav case, 'humanitarianism alone is not capable of stopping human hardship. We must find peaceful political solutions to conflicts.' Until that point of awareness is reached which will make it possible to restore justice and transform societies, humanitarian aid will be necessary to help many people through a critical period.

Proposals

- More participation in aid by countries that have supplied weapons.
- Training of civilian and military specialists for relief operations and protection of refugees.
- Create a United Nations force specialising in the protection and distribution of relief supplies.
- Increase UNHCR resources.
- Set up sapper units available to the United Nations for mine clearance.
- Transfer part of the military information and telecommunications systems to humanitarian uses.
- Reconstruct damaged infrastructure so that relief can enter the country.
- Set up a permanent air, land and sea transport force available to the UN.
- Make national military bases and installations available for use in relief operations.

5

The Peace-Keeping Forces

Almost since its very foundation, the United Nations has intervened, though with very variable results, in the prevention and pacification of certain conflicts, by sending Observation Missions (the 'blue berets') or Peace-keeping Forces (PKFs), commonly known as 'blue helmets'.

The Observation Missions are made up of observers or professional military liaison officers, who are unarmed and whose duty it is to passively supervise and observe the fulfilment of the Security Council's mandate. The PKFs are equipped with light defensive arms. They are usually complete units (battalions or companies) from different countries and act rather more decisively, though without joining combat, with the object of dissuading the parties involved in the conflict.

The official in charge of these United Nations operations has redefined PKFs as 'those United Nations operations in which civil or military personnel take part, with the consent of the parties involved and under the orders of the United Nations, to help control and resolve international conflicts or internal conflicts, real or potential, which have a clear international dimension'.[1] The basic characteristics of these operations are as follows:

- They take place with the agreement of the hostile parties.
- Each operation has the approval and support of the United Nations (it needs the affirmative vote of at least 9 of the 15 members of the Security Council).
- The military personnel are volunteers and belong to the governments taking part.
- This military personnel is under the orders of the Secretary General, who reports to the Security Council.
- Peace-keeping Operations (PKOs) are impartial.
- Force is not normally used. If it is used it is kept to a minimum.
- The operations must be paid for by the Member States.

For 40 years, and until very recently, the operations in which these forces have taken part consisted of surveillance in the initial or the final stages of conflicts, either to prevent escalation (the preventive role), to monitor a cease-fire or troop withdrawal or as an element of interposition to achieve a negotiated end to hostilities. PKFs have therefore acted as a police force in charge of maintaining order at a delicate moment in which the presence of an impartial outside force can guarantee the fulfilment of certain agreements.

However, this tradition came to an end with the operation in Somalia. Indeed, for the first time in the history of PKOs, the United Nations tried to combine in one operation a humanitarian project and a military offensive. At the time of writing, the results are frankly negative, with the military side interfering with the humanitarian side and even with the political side, showing the difficulty or even impossibility of doing the two things at once.

Somalia has also been a test bed for a new kind of peace-force, the so-called forces of 'imposition', which combine traditional elements with others of a more offensive type. It seemed too dangerous to try them out in Yugoslavia; in Somalia it was easier and, what is more, it could be legitimated before public opinion with pictures of starving children. However, events have shown that it is all far more complicated and that in the final instance the United Nations cannot be judge and party. Hence the criticism of the offensive nature of the operation in Somalia (UNOSOM) acquired after a certain point, something which has been interpreted as a critical transformation in the role of the United Nations, which went from being a mediator in the process of national reconciliation to being an active belligerent.

As opposed to a short list of successes, the failure of other operations is also evident. Bertrand, influenced by the pessimism provoked by successive crises accumulated during 1993, summed it up as follows:

In Angola (where there was hope of success until the day Savimbi lost the elections); in Afghanistan, where the civil war is getting more and more destructive; in Cambodia, where the Khmer Rouge still refuse to co-operate; in former Yugoslavia, where the war goes on over the heads of the 'blue helmets' and negotiations are trampled on; in Somalia, where the factions have lost none of their aggressiveness (and the United States operate on their own account) ... Political interventions, for their part, are not bringing solutions in the Near East, or in Cyprus, or in the Western Sahara, or in Cashmere or in Haiti.[2]

The absence of positive results in a number of operations which have not managed to provide a definitive solution to conflicts has a lot to do with the limited preventive capacity of the United Nations itself, the lack of clear criteria for reaching political agreement between rival parties, ignorance of the historical context and the social reality of the area of operations, confusion between 'peace-keeping' and 'peace-enforcement', poor preparation, total unsuitability or lack of neutrality on the part of some of the people taking part in operations, and the lateness of the action of the Organisation as a whole, which is similar to that of a fireman arriving at the fire when the building has already been destroyed.[3]

From the moment the Security Council studies the possibility of sending observers or establishing a PKO, until it is actually established, a few days can go by (as in the case of Georgia) or half a year (Liberia, Cambodia or Somalia). This is lost time during which the situation can deteriorate irremediably. Furthermore, the actual deployment of military forces usually takes place several months after the operation is formally launched.

Pacifying conflicts that have been going on for 10 or 20 years can never be easy unless it includes a wide range of measures which take the root of the problem into consideration. It makes little sense that some PKOs should last indefinitely or that they should be prematurely brought to an end. Ideally, they should last just as long as is strictly necessary, but without an approach that facilitates their perpetuity due to adaptation by the conflicting parties. At the present moment there are four operations that have been going on for more than 20 years (Palestine, India/Pakistan, Cyprus and the Golan Heights) and another that has been going on for more than 16 (Lebanon). Not counting the operations begun after the first half of 1993, so far only six PKOs (a fifth of the total) have lasted less than a year.

Obviously, the best solution would be a preventive deployment of PKFs, before the conflict reached a certain level. So far, however, the United Nations has done little in the preventive stages and changing this attitude would mean also acting on the economic and social causes which produce these conflictive situations and not only on their military manifestations. This is Boutros Boutros-Ghali's view when he says that 'the efforts of the Organisation to consolidate peace, stability and security must encompass subjects which go beyond military threats, so as to make it possible to break the chain of conflicts and wars which have characterised the past'.[4] It is worth remembering, though, that the Peace Forces will never be able to solve conflicts by themselves, and even less so the long-term conflicts. Solving conflicts calls for the adoption of additional mechanisms, more along the lines of what the United Nations Secretary General calls 'peace building'. PKOs in their present form can be of use in bringing to an end a process of reduction of tensions between states, rather than being their forerunner.[5]

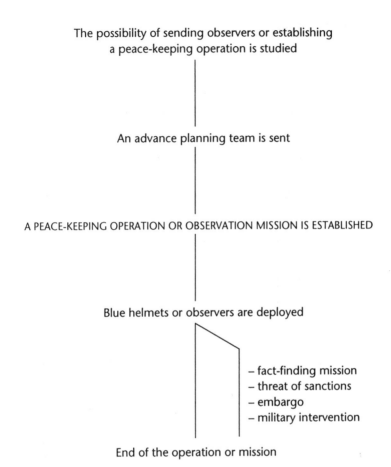

Figure 5.1 The process of a peace-keeping operation

The relative failure of some of these operations also has an explanation in the concept of 'peace-keeping' originally established by the victors of the Second World War, whose chief concern was to maintain the new balance of powers as well as their own privileges.[6] As Bertrand, who has a good inside knowledge of the United Nations, points out, peace-keeping operations were used for 30 years, from 1948 to 1978, to stabilise the situation in the Middle East (four operations in the Israeli sphere and one in Cyprus) or to solve embarrassing problems in the old colonial powers, but never to solve the many Cold War conflicts. Since 1987, he adds, in spite of its apparent growth the role of the United Nations in matters of security has been

Table 5.1 Mandates granted to United Nations forces

Mandate	Haiti	Liberia	Georgia	Rwanda	Somalia	Mozambique	Former Yugoslavia	El Salvador	Cambodia	Angola
Contacts with conflicting parties			•	•						
Mediation to bring about cease-fire agreements		•	•	•	•	•	•	•	•	•
Supervising, verifying or maintaining agreements (cease-fires, etc.)				•						
Monitoring situations and reporting to the SG										
Border surveillance to verify non-arrival of military assistance					•		•			
Surveillance of arms embargoes				•			•			
Contributing to safety in cities							•			
Preventing attacks on safety zones					•					
Supervising a country's safety situation							•			
Occupying key points					•		•			
Protecting ports, airports or lines of communication										
Establishing demilitarised or unarmed zones							•			
Supervising armed forces quartering, meeting-points or withdrawal		•		•	•	•	•		•	
Supervising armed forces disarmament or demobilisation		•		•					•	
Storage and surveillance of weapons and military equipment										
Supervising integration of armed forces										
Training for mine-clearance		•		•	•	•			•	
Providing training for armed forces in non-aggressive techniques	•			•						
Guaranteeing prohibition of military flights over certain regions							•			
Use of airforce to defend safety zones							•			

Table 5.1 *continued*

Activity	Haiti	Liberia	Georgia	Rwanda	Somalia	Mozambique	Former Yugoslavia	El Salvador	Cambodia	Angola
Assistance in re-establishing police forces					•			•		
Providing guidance and advice on policing	•								•	•
Investigating and reporting on non-compliance or violation of agreements		•	•	•					•	
Investigating and reporting on violations of human rights			•					•		•
Investigating incidents involving police forces				•						
Arrest and trial of criminals					•					
Promoting reconciliation processes and political settlements					•				•	
Restoring civilian administration institutions					•	•			•	
Drawing up human rights educational programmes									•	
Reorganising the judicial system										
Assisting political processes in progress					•				•	
Education and preparation for electoral processes					•				•	
Observing and verifying political processes		•							•	•
Creating the right conditions for participation by the civilian society					•					
Providing public information on PKO activities					•	•		•		
Providing security and protection for civilians, refugees or displaced people				•	•				•	
Providing protection for NGO personnel					•					
Establishing safe humanitarian areas				•						
Providing urgent humanitarian aid and ensuring delivery of relief supplies					•		•			

Table 5.1 *continued*

	Helping in humanitarian aid activities and relief operations	Providing protection and support for aid distribution	Protecting convoys of released prisoners	Help in liberating prisoners of war	Help in economic reconstruction and rehabilitation	Help in restoring public services in safety zones
Haiti						
Liberia						
Georgia	•					
Rwanda		•				
Somalia	•	•			•	
Mozambique	•					
Former Yugoslavia	•	•	•			•
El Salvador	•					
Cambodia				•		
Angola						

limited to three functions: giving its name to a North-American initiative in the Gulf (and since then 'joining in' its unilateral decisions, such as the attack on Somalia in July 1993); playing the part of a fireman and putting out fires after they have almost entirely destroyed certain countries (Afghanistan, Western Sahara, Angola); freeing the large powers of the tedious management of unsolvable issues (Western Sahara, Cyprus, Yugoslavia).[7]

Although the present situation is very different from that of only ten years ago, the same philosophy of keeping order still holds, a remnant of the Cold War, incapable of confronting the security problems of the modern world.

The fact is that as time goes by PKOs tend to become more frequent, complex and ambitious, and there is already talk of a 'second generation of peace-keeping [which] is certain to involve not only military but also political, economic, social, humanitarian and environmental dimensions, all in need of a unified and integrated approach'.[8]

Until 1990, the United Nations PKOs centred on missions of interposition and border surveillance or fulfilled policing functions monitoring cease-fires, troop withdrawal and, more recently, electoral processes.

Table 5.2 Mandates of the last ten PKOs

	No. PKOs
Supervision of cease-fire agreements	8
Supervision of disarmament, demobilisation truce or troop withdrawal	6
Overseeing electoral processes	5
Humanitarian assistance	5
Mine clearance	5
Investigation of infringements of agreements or violations of human rights	5
Policing	4
Surveillance of embargoes and preventing arrival of military aid	3
Promotion of political reconciliation	3
Protection of refugees and displaced people	3

Since 1991, however, Security Council mandates for some ten new missions have not only considerably enlarged the traditional role of the 'blue helmets', but have given a false sensation that the

United Nations can do everything, when in fact it is not yet in a position to satisfactorily carry out certain very complex high-risk missions for the simple reason that the states making up the United Nations have not assimilated certain duties and obligations arising from the approbation of these mandates.

The observable tendency of the last few years has been to maintain traditional mandates to monitor cease-fire agreements, demobilisation and electoral processes, but with the addition on various occasions of the work of disarming conflicting parties, providing or protecting humanitarian assistance, investigating infringement of cease-fire agreements or violations of human rights, monitoring oil and arms embargoes, preventing arms from crossing borders and protecting refugees and displaced people.

The operations in Somalia, former Yugoslavia, Cambodia and Rwanda, regardless of results, have been the cause of this expansion in the mandates, all of them accumulating up to 16 simultaneous objectives as opposed to the two or three objectives established in slightly earlier operations. In view of this, it is worth asking ourselves if the mandates of these more recent operations have not exceeded the true possibilities and capacities of the troops taking part in them, and if some military mandates are compatible with others of a more political or humanitarian nature.

As Human Rights Watch said:

human rights have been treated as a dispensable luxury, not as a central element in the success of United Nations peacekeeping and humanitarian operations. The cost of this inattention to human rights is anything but academic. It can be measured in damaged credibility, operational missteps and impaired effectiveness ... The effect of this disregard is also felt in the squandered opportunities and diminished prospects for success of United Nations field operations. Because abuses such as murder, torture and deliberate starvation fuel the crises that the United Nations is attempting to overcome, the failure to end those abuses and to establish a system of accountability that will deter their recurrence leaves a shaky foundation on which to build long-term security.[9]

In this sense, the United Nations must organise the operations in accordance with Amnesty International's 15-point programme for implementing human rights in international peace-keeping operations.[10]

Table 5.3 Amnesty International's 15-point programme

Point

---

1. The United Nations and its Member States should give early, consistent and vigorous attention to human rights concerns when designing and implementing peace settlements and should plan for a continued human rights program in the post-peace-keeping phase.
2. All international field personnel, including those engaged in military, civilian and humanitarian operations, should report through explicit and proper channels any human rights violations they may witness or serious allegations they receive.
3. Peace settlement should require eventual ratification of any human rights treaties and adherence to any international system of human rights protection to which the state concerned is not yet a party.
4. A specialised international civilian human rights monitoring component should be part of all peace-keeping operations. Their mandates should include human rights verification, institution-building, legislative reform, education and training.
5. Peace settlements should provide for impartial investigation of past abuses.
6. Human rights monitors should have broad access to all sectors of society and relevant institutions and the full protection of those who are in contact with them must be assured.
7. Human rights personnel. There must be frequent comprehensive public reports of their activities and findings which should be broadly disseminated nationally as well as internationally.
8. Civilian police monitors should monitor, supervise and train national police and security forces and verify their adherence to international human rights and criminal justice standards.
9. Human rights components in peace-keeping operations should assist in the establishment of permanent, independent and effective national institutions for the long-term protection of human rights and the reinstitution of the rule of law, including an independent judiciary and fair criminal justice system.
10. Public education and training on human rights standards and complaints procedures should be provided to all sectors, particularly the judiciary, lawyers and law enforcement officials.
11. Refugee repatriation programs should include an effective monitoring and protection aspect for as long as necessary.
12. Measures should be taken to guarantee consideration and respect for the particular needs of women in armed conflict situations. Peace-keeping personnel should receive information on local cultural traditions and should respect the inherent rights and dignity of women at all times.
13. The United Nations should ensure all troops participating in international peace-keeping operations are fully trained in those standards and understand their obligation to adhere to them. There should be specific mechanisms at the international level for monitoring, investigating and reporting on any violations of international norms by peace-keeping personnel.
14. The investigation and prosecution of violations of humanitarian and human rights law or attacks against international peace-keeping personnel should be undertaken by appropiate national authorities or under international jurisdiction.
15. Effective international human rights monitoring and assistance should be continued for as long as necessary, until it is clear that the government concerned is implementing international human rights guarantees effectively.

The tragic case of Rwanda is quite significant. In August 1993, the Security Council approved the establishment of UNOMUR, made up of 81 military observers with the mission of verifying that military assistance was not reaching Rwanda via the border with Uganda. This border was a weak point through which the FPR were introducing arms and troops without difficulty. On 16 June 1994, the United Nations Secretary General reported that UNOMUR could not watch over the 170 km of border between Rwanda and Uganda since it only had seven control posts and three helicopters. But it went on to say that 'so far there is no evidence of a significant traffic in arms or movement of military personnel', something quite extraordinary if we remember that in the previous paragraph it was recognised that UNOMUR did not have sufficient means to control the border, and that by that time the advance of the FPR had already led half a million Rwandans to take refuge in neighbouring countries.

Even more dramatic is the case of UNAMIR, the mission set up in Rwanda in October 1993, which integrated the previous mission UNOMUR and whose mandate was to contribute to security in the city of Kigali, supervise the cease-fire and security in the country until the elections, help to clear mines, investigate infringements of the Arusha Agreement on the integration of the armed forces, supervise the process of repatriation, help co-ordinate the humanitarian assistance and investigate incidents connected with the activities of the gendarmerie and the police. Three months later, UNAMIR and UNOMUR consisted of 1,687 troops, of which 934 were from Bangladesh and 430 from Belgium. The question is simple: was it really possible to carry out all these mandates with these troops, from 22 different countries, of which more than half were Bangladeshi, only 14 per cent were African and very few spoke French, Swahili or Kinyarwanda? Whatever the case, subsequent events have shown for themselves the total inability of these troops to carry out any of the jobs entrusted to them.

A quarter of the mandates of the ten operations begun since 1991, furthermore, refer to aspects involving the use of military force or making it very likely (monitoring embargoes, providing security in cities, protecting security areas, occupying key points, protecting infrastructures and communications lines, surveillance of confiscated arms, ensuring the prohibition of military flights, protecting NGOs and the distribution of humanitarian aid, etc.). The dissuasive or force element of PKOs is increasingly present in the mandates approved by the Security Council, which makes growing use of Chapter VII of the Charter to back up its decisions. In 1993, Chapter VII was used on 20 occasions and in six countries to impose sanctions or embargoes or to authorise the use of force in different circumstances. In the first half of 1994, Chapter VII has served to justify the adoption of similar measures on eight occasions.

This increase in the use of force, however, has not been accompanied either by a greater provision of the United Nations' resources for putting it into practice, or by international debate on the scope and the consequences of this use of force. This establishes the dangerous precedent of the Security Council making empty threats, so that in the absence of permanently available forces specially trained for acting in PKOs, it has to beg Member States for troops or request intervention by those military powers prepared to play the part of a global police force.

Curiously enough, the operation in which the mandates are most military in nature is the one in former Yugoslavia (UNPROFOR), and not, as one might suppose, the ones in Somalia (UNOSOM) or Rwanda (UNAMIR–UNOMUR). In view of what has actually happened, though, one can only assume that there are some operations in which the military activity has exceeded the strict limits of the Security Council mandate and others in which the inevitable military activity has perhaps not been sufficiently calibrated at the beginning of the operation.

One of the lessons to be learnt from the PKOs of the last few years is precisely the need to clarify and spell out the mandates for operations so as to avoid confusion and misunderstanding. Another conclusion is that the mandates must reflect what is really going to happen and not something we would like to see happen but know to be impossible. A realistic mandate, though limited and modest, can provide security for those carrying it out and those receiving it; an unrealistic mandate, on the other hand, will in all certainty create frustration.

There are even proposals, though not yet very detailed ones, for extending the field of action of the United Nations forces to the ecological sphere. The UNESCO Secretary General, Federico Mayor Zaragoza, has repeatedly suggested the creation of 'green helmets' devoted to ecological prevention and protection. Norway even plans to create a body of 'green troops' linked to the United Nations Centre for Urgent Environmental Aid, which would be educated and trained to provide aid in natural disasters and oil or chemical spillages. For the time being, and as a possible step in that direction, there has, since 1993, been a Court of Environmental Affairs at the International Court of Justice, made up of seven magistrates.

The constant enlargement of the field of action of the PKFs is both a necessity, responding to a real demand, and a serious threat to their future if their functions, limits and means are not spelled out very soon. The PKFs are having to confront very different situations to those of the immediate past – or they are being asked to – without the necessary political discussion having taken place to correctly define the role of the United Nations in these situations and of course the object of its peace forces.

The Position of the United States

The level of future involvement which the United States decides it wants to have in the general running of the United Nations will to a large extent condition the approach to PKOs in the coming years. The war in the Gulf and the intervention in Somalia have been two important test beds in this field, and although the military nature of the two conflicts differs substantially from the traditional task of the United Nations PKOs, their outcome and the impact on the public have forced a reconsideration of the United States' traditional position of aloofness from the United Nations, and its replacement by a more active, though conditioned, attitude.

In May 1993, a report by the president of the Congress Foreign Relations Committee, Lee H. Hamilton, on North-American foreign policy in the post-Cold War era[11] recommended reinforcing the work of the United Nations in collective security, admitting Japan and Germany as permanent members of the Security Council, enlarging the Security Council to include more representatives of the Third World, establishing a professional military command structure in the United Nations, accepting the fact that some offensive PKOs are necessary, reducing and rationalising the American contribution to these operations, more actively supporting PKOs from the Defense Department and training North-American forces specially designated to intervene in them. It also recommended that the North-American troops taking part in multilateral missions should remain under North-American command if there is a chance of their being involved in hostilities. Troop deployment should always be authorised by Congress, and in the case of hostilities the United States should maintain control of the operations.

In August of the same year, Clinton signed a directive on PKOs[12] stating that the United States supported a rapid expansion of these operations in the world, although it did not accept Boutros Boutros-Ghali's proposal that the United Nations should have rapid deployment forces of its own. According to this directive, the United States would accept United Nations command of the operations and that its troops should be put under the 'operational control' of the

United Nations command, but ordered North-American officers to maintain independent channels of information with the top American military authorities and authorised North-American officers to disobey any United Nations order they judged to be illegal or 'militarily unwise', a highly ambiguous term which shows up the United States' reluctance to submit to the military command of any other country.

That same month, a report by the Senate Committee on Foreign Relations[13] also recommended a change in United States policy regarding PKOs, with the introduction of specific measures to overcome the legal and administrative obstacles limiting North-American participation in these United Nations operations, and negotiation of the special agreements foreseen in Article 43 of the Charter so as to provide operations with rapid assistance, supply the United Nations with modern communications material, allow the deployment of North-American combat troops under the command of the United Nations, train them specifically for these operations, reduce the United States' economic contribution to the same level as its regular quota (25 per cent), and set up an emergency fund for those PKOs in which North-American troops take part.

The report's recommendation therefore represents a step forward in the involvement of the United States in the peace-keeping work of the United Nations, though with conditions, and without hiding the fact that one of the reasons for increasing their presence in PKOs is to counter the current leadership of other countries, and of France in particular.

At the beginning of September 1993, Secretary of Defense Les Aspin presented a report on the future structure of the United States military forces[14] which included a section headed 'Peace Enforcement and Intervention Operations', clearly influenced by the experiences of Iraq, Somalia and former Yugoslavia, spelling out certain details of North-American collaboration with the United Nations or other international organisations, with the following five objectives in mind:

- to reach and keep open access to airports, ports and other installations;
- to control troop movements and positions on the borders of the target country and ensure a commercial blockade;
- to establish and defend areas in which the civilian population will be protected from external attacks;
- to provide security in areas to be protected from internal threats such as snipers, terrorist attacks and sabotage; and

- to prepare the transfer of responsibility in security matters to peace-keeping units or to a reconstituted administrative authority.

The Defense Department's report gives details for the first time of the 'wise' level of forces that should be planned for intervention in these operations, namely:

- 1 air assault or airborne division
- 1 light infantry division
- 1 Marine Expeditionary Brigade
- 1–2 carrier battle groups
- 1–2 composite wings of Air Force aircraft
- Special operations forces
- Civil affairs units
- Airlift and sealift forces
- Combat support and service support units

The forces assigned to these operations, whether for combat or support missions, would amount to 50,000 troops and would have to be prepared to act in the case of the United States being simultaneously engaged in two important regional conflicts, in accordance with the new 'two and a half wars' strategy[15] (also known as 'Option C'), favoured by Defense Secretary Les Aspin himself, and which aims at being able to take on simultaneously a war like the one in the Gulf and two lesser contingencies of a regional type.

In the revised structure of the Pentagon, the units are reorganised under four types of force: strategic, contingency, Atlantic and Pacific. The field of action of the last two covers Europe/Middle East and East Asia respectively. The contingency forces would provide the initial troops for rapid deployment in any part of the planet. The annual cost of all these intervention forces is estimated at $195,000 million ($66,000 for the Atlantic, $44,000 for the Pacific, $38,000 for the contingency forces and $47,000 for the additional support),[16] 50 times the annual cost of all the United Nations PKOs. The planning and infrastructure for unilateral interventions in any part of the world therefore remains standing, even in this post-Cold War period.

The future of PKOs and the reform of the United Nations were also present in President Clinton's first speech before the United Nations General Assembly on 27 September 1993.[17] Clinton said that although United States soldiers were ready to act in United Nations missions (availability), they cannot take part in all the world's conflicts (selectivity). He also stressed that the United Nations must be absolutely clear as to its limitations (realism) and must reduce its bureaucracy and its spending. Clinton, like Bush a year earlier, committed himself to negotiating with Congress payment of the $800 million owed to the United Nations, although in exchange he asked for a reduction in the quota.

Table 5.4 Financing peace-keeping missions, 1995

	% regular budget	% peace-keeping budget
United States	25.00	31.15
Japan	13.95	14.00
Germany	8.94	8.98
France	6.32	7.87
Russian Fed.	5.68	7.08
United Kingdom	5.27	6.57

Source: United Nations, ST/ADM/SER. B/463, 8 February 1995

In addition, in September and October of that year there was a real campaign to publicise North America's new foreign policy on the part of its maximum representatives. In all the speeches, whether by Clinton himself[18] or by Secretary of State Warren Christopher,[19] United States United Nations ambassador Madeleine Albright[20] or National Security Advisor Anthony Lake,[21] the memory of Somalia and, in the more recent speeches, the problem of Haiti, which has already suffered the 'Somalia syndrome', are ever present. The approach to the United Nations, the pragmatism of accepting both multilateralism and unilateralism depending on the circumstances and North-American interests, the simplification of the exterior discourse to two concepts (democracy and market), the use of humanitarianism as a strategy to stimulate these concepts, the insistence on or obsession with maintaining leadership, and the repeated warning that force will be used unilaterally when necessary, are some of the key elements of this policy, which is also summed up in the statement: 'in short, the United States views peace operations as a means to support our national security strategy, not as a strategy unto itself'.[22]

From an analysis of these reports and declarations, we can deduce, first of all, that the gap between peace-keeping operations and operations using force (or peace-imposition operations) is getting smaller and smaller in North-American thinking, which inevitably leads to confusion as to the United Nations' mission in this field. The policies favoured by the Clinton administration seem to be directed at getting active and effective control of the United Nations, as opposed to the 'passive control' (by means of its veto and its economic stranglehold) exerted during the Cold War. In this way, the United Nations becomes the instrument which has to provide legitimacy and cover for future military interventions, which would also have the blessing of the enlarged Security Council, in which the presence of Japan and Germany would ensure an equitable distribution of the financial cost of these operations and a greater involvement of the NATO allies, both on a financial level and in human resources, because, as Pelanda has pointed out,[23] 'the United States has an objective interest in constructing a system of collective administration of international security which would involve distributing the cost, whether military or to encourage peace, while at the same time retaining its leadership'.

The speech by Ambassador Albright before the Senate Foreign Relations Committee is especially significant in that it publicly recognises North America's change of heart in the operation in Somalia, its acceptance of a greater emphasis on political reconciliation within the country, and less on the military element, and that it took place at a moment of North-American unrest over the delicate situation in Haiti, which calls for care if recent errors are not to be repeated. This care, though a result of circumstances, reinforces the United States' tentative position as regards United Nations PKOs, which Albright spells out in the following terms:

- The PKFs need more training and better equipment.
- The North-American contribution should be mainly in the sphere of logistics, intelligence and communications, rather than in combat.
- They will only fight under North-American command or, as a last resort, under the command of someone from NATO considered fully trustworthy.
- In operations on a large scale (like the war in the Gulf) or entailing a high risk (like Somalia), United Nations leadership is unlikely to be accepted. The United States will base itself on its own resources.
- Whatever the case, a North-American chain of command will always be maintained parallel to that of the UN.

The United States, then, resorts to double-talk as regards the use of force by the United Nations. On one hand, it supports the creation within the United Nations of a true general headquarters for PKOs, with access to the necessary intelligence, communications and logistics (proposal by Clinton before the General Assembly), but at the same time they demand a revision of the decision-making process of the PKOs, American command of the operations in which it intervenes, and in this last case, 'the existence of a clear mission, with competent commanders, reasonable rules of conduct, and the necessary means to carry out the work'. These are all common-sense demands and will in all certainty be shared by all those countries which have had experience in the most difficult PKOs. Nevertheless, the problem, and one which causes understandable misgivings, lies in the somewhat arrogant condition that 'we'll only go if we're in charge', which goes against the essence of the PKOs, which should always reflect the multinational, participative and co-operative nature of their structure, as well as their dependence on the United Nations. If every country adopted the same attitude as the United States, it quite simply would not be possible to organise another Peace-keeping Operation.

Present and Future of the PKOs

If this takeover of the United Nations, by means of a transformation of the traditional PKOs into a form of legal intervention, goes ahead, the concept of collective security will no longer be a valid designation for the 'shared' nature of security, since it will only represent the interests of the more powerful, finally united around the same table in the Security Council.

The possibility that this new Security Council will have political, economic and strategic dominion over the planet does not mean either that it will have the necessary resources or mechanisms to regulate the conflicts of today's society and guarantee an acceptable level of global security. The end of the Cold War has led to a transformation in conflicts by releasing the brakes of USA–USSR competition and unleashing a wide range of regional tensions. With the disintegration of states, the existence of two contradictory tendencies has come to light: globalisation on one hand and fragmentation or retribalisation on the other. In Europe, the emergence of new states raises numerous disputes over minorities and borders. In the Third World, furthermore, violence arises largely through long-lasting local factors, many of them a result of the colonial period. The great majority of today's conflicts are not conventional wars but internal ethnic or political conflicts. The peace-keeping operations of the last few years are themselves evidence of this, since ten of the 13 operations begun since 1988 have had as their goal the resolution of internal conflicts and a transition to more democratic political systems.[24]

The nature and the dynamics of these conflicts are highly complex, which makes them difficult to handle and regulate by outside organisations using totally inappropriate methods. Traditional defence policies are anyway not prepared for this type of conflict, many of which have entered a vicious circle of political, ideological and ethnic antagonism, which has got out of control. As a study by Médecins Sans Frontières says:

> these conflicts have become a way of life and have found in themselves the fuel for their own reproduction. Over the ruins of the State and in the absence of arbitration, they become privatised, criminalised and permanently restructured on the basis of a predatory economy fed by plunder and trafficking of all kinds.[25]

and as Enzensberger so rightly says:

> the civil wars of our days break out spontaneously, from within. They no longer have need of foreign powers to reach conflict escalation ... All these self-proclaimed popular liberation armies, movements and fronts have degenerated into marauding bands who are hardly any different from their opponents.[26]

Their members usually have the autistic nature of criminals and set out to eliminate the defenceless. In short, a polemical context, in which the blue helmets have a good chance of being misunderstood and of being violently rejected by one part of the population.

We must not forget that in these internal conflicts the distinction between combatants and non-combatants no longer holds and the immense majority of victims are civilians. Whereas in the conflicts of the 1950s half of the victims belonged to the civilian population, in the 1980s this figure rose to three-quarters, and it is estimated that today civilians account for 90 per cent of victims.[27]

Can the United Nations arbitrate in situations of this type? Can its peace forces intervene with any chance of success, even with the knowledge that these are structural conflicts, impossible to solve in the short term, or that they require political changes, perhaps even in the international system?

In his *Agenda for Peace*, Boutros Boutros-Ghali refers to three types of case in which preventive deployment of the PKFs is possible:

- In situations of national crisis, at the request of the government or of all the parties involved, or with their consent (aid to conciliation, humanitarian assistance, help in maintaining security).

- In disputes between states, when two countries consider that a United Nations presence on either side of the border could reduce the risk of hostilities.
- When a country considers itself threatened.

Although the PKFs can only act with the consent of the rival parties, the third case allows the possibility of preventive intervention in a country even when this is not to the liking of a third party. But the PKFs are in no case authorised to intervene in a state's internal affairs without the consent of the government. Nevertheless, and following the experiences of the intervention in Somalia and Iraqi Kurdistan, several doubts arise as to the interpretation of when an 'internal affair' also becomes an 'external affair', or, following the terms of Article 2(7) of the Charter, when an 'affair belongs essentially to the internal jurisdiction of States'. These doubts are due to two causes:[28]

- Civil conflicts within a country can have repercussions abroad, either because they directly affect other countries, or because the refugees caused by the conflict threaten or destabilise neighbouring countries. The cases of former Yugoslavia, Somalia and Kurdistan are examples of this.
- The application of international law for the protection of human rights means that the United Nations must intervene to guarantee the security of peoples, and not of states.

There is every reason to believe that the Security Council will increase its participation in solutions to conflicts previously considered internal, which are the majority, normally on humanitarian grounds. It is therefore foreseeable that the PKFs will be transformed so as to adapt them to these situations, under their old name or a new one.

From the signing of the United Nations Charter in June 1945, until April 1994 – that is, in 49 years – some 650,000 people in 75 countries have served in these United Nations operations, including military, civilian and policing operations, with a total cost of some $10,400 million. More than 1,100 people have lost their lives serving in these forces, most of them on missions still in progress.

Although at first sight these figures might seem very high, we must remember that in the same period of time the world's military forces have mobilised more than 1,000 million people, as opposed to the 650,000 of the peace forces, and that global military expenditure has exceeded $30,000,000 million ($30 billion). In other words, since the Second World War, for each 'blue helmet' there have been 1,600 'khaki helmets', and for each 'blue' dollar spent, $3,000 have been assigned to the 'khakis'. Even in recent years, in which the cost of all the Peace-keeping Operations has been considerably higher than in previous times, it has not exceeded the cost of two days of Operation 'Desert Storm', in which Japan alone invested more than $12,000 million. Historically, therefore, the dice have not rolled in favour of the Peace-keeping Forces, but of preparation for war and the strengthening of the military forces in charge of waging it.

Table 5.5 Comparison of peace-keeping operations expenditure and world military expenditure, 1993

Peace-keeping Operations spending ($ millions)	3,600
World military expenditure ($ millions)	920,000
% Peace-keeping cost/military expenditure	0.4
Military personnel in Peace-keeping Operations	76,500
World armed forces	28,000,000
% Peace-keeping forces/world armed forces	0.3

There is nevertheless reason to believe that this enormous disparity between military forces and peace forces could change in the future, even if only very little. The growing demand for intervention by United Nations forces in a range of conflictive situations all over the world and the increase in operations and personnel since the end of the 1980s, leading to the point of collapse in 1993, at least calls for a debate on the future of these forces and a clarification of the role they will have to play in the context of a United Nations in transformation.

Between 1948 and 1994, the United Nations carried out 34 Peace-keeping Operations. What is significant, though, is that in the first 39 years, that is between 1948 and 1987, 13 operations were started, an average of one every three years. In the following five-year period, that is between 1988 and 1993, 20 new operations were begun, an average of four a year and a rate twelve times that of the earlier period. The requests for new operations are continuous. It is enough to point out that in just the four months from October 1992 to January 1993 the United Nations Secretary General received demands for intervention in Abjazia (a secessionist territory of Georgia), Mozambique, Macedonia, Iraqi Kurdistan, Liberia, Bosnia and Herzegovina and Haiti.[29] Some of them have been answered and others will have to wait uncertainly in line. What is obvious is that in a world with insufficient mechanisms for regulating conflicts, the United Nations is seen as a possible last hope or as a mitigating element for a large number of high-tension situations, but unfortunately it lacks the means, the moral legitimacy or the attributions to effectively intervene in all the scenarios calling for its presence.

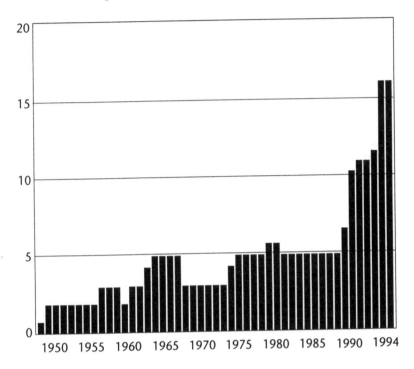

Figure 5.2 Peace-keeping, number of operations

At the end of 1994, the United Nations had 16 operations in progress, in which more than 76,000 people were taking part, with an annual budget of $3,600 million. Four years earlier, the personnel involved was one-seventh the size.

The operation in former Yugoslavia, with 40,000 troops in September 1994, is the one involving the largest number of military forces. It is followed by the operation in Somalia, which mobilised 26,000 troops, and the one in Cambodia, with 22,000. These three operations involved a deployment unprecedented in the history of the PKOs, if we exclude the mission to the Congo in 1961, in which almost 20,000 men took part. Apart from these cases, the largest United Nations missions have never exceeded the figure of 7,000 troops.

Table 5.6 Personnel involved in peace-keeping operations

October	1985	9,771
June	1990	10,749
November	1992	47,915
March	1993	49,501
June	1993	77,310
October	1993	76,680
January	1994	70,150
March	1994	68,463
May	1994	68,936
June	1994	71,543
September	1994	76,111

Table 5.7 Most important PKF deployments (*)

Operation	Country	Maximum deployment	Date
UNPROFOR	former Yugoslavia	39,922	September 94
UNOSOM	Somalia	26,112	October 93
UNTAC	Cambodia	22,000	March 93
ONUC	Congo	19,828	July 61
UNEF II	Sinai	6,973	February 74
ONUMOZ	Mozambique	6,843	March 94
UNFICYP	Cyprus	6,411	June 64
UNEF I	Sinai	6,073	February 57
UNIFIL	Lebanon	5,904	June 90
UNTAG	Namibia	4,493	November 89

(*) Situation as at September 1994.

The complexity and the nature of many operations (observation of the fulfilment of human rights, supervision of new administrations, electoral information and surveillance, specialists in refugees, humanitarian aid, policing, etc.) means that there is growing participation by civilian personnel in the PKFs, often in a role as important or more so than the military forces. In the year 1992 alone, the United Nations provided technical assistance for elections in Albania, Angola, the Congo, El Salvador, Ethiopia, Guinea, Guyana, Liberia, Madagascar, Mali, Rwanda and Togo. Since the Office of Electoral Assistance of the Department of Political Affairs of the Secretariat has been in existence, the United Nations has provided electoral assistance to 36 Member States, 26 of them African. To

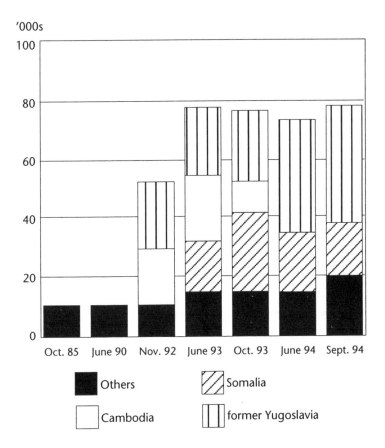

'000s

Figure 5.3 Peace-keeping forces

improve the training and qualification of this personnel, the United Nations ought to draw up agreements with certain countries so that international training courses in this subject could be provided for civilian personnel at specialised centres.

To the significant participation of civilian personnel in the PKOs we must add the invaluable collaboration of numerous non-governmental organisations in operations to provide humanitarian aid, repatriate refugees or protect human rights. This civilian presence could be increased in the future if the proposal made in October 1992 by the UNESCO Executive Committee gets off the ground. The proposal is for programmes for a culture of peace for areas of conflict where the PKFs are deployed, although the uncertainty or failure of

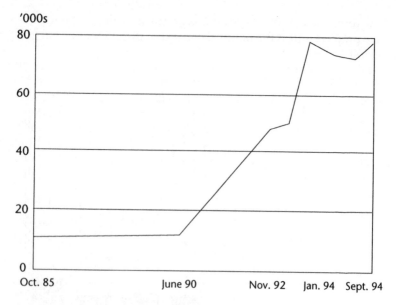

Figure 5.4 Personnel involved in PKOs

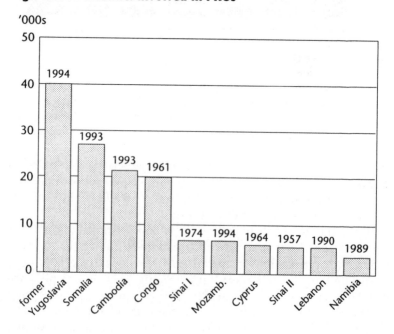

Figure 5.5 The biggest deployments

some recent operations casts doubts on the possibility of beginning these projects unless the political context of the operations has been previously resolved.

The list of countries that have taken part in PKOs reflects the differences in the degree of co-operation in international issues. The countries with the best record of participation in PKOs tend to be neutral or non-aligned, economically developed countries with small populations, a high level of political freedom, open and active foreign policies and reduced military expenditure, which stand out for their policy of co-operation with the Third World, a description matching the principles which in theory preside over the actions of the United Nations.

Sweden,[30] Canada,[31] Ireland, Austria and Norway, in that order, are the countries that have taken part in most operations since 1980.[32] Of the five, three are neutral, four have less than ten million inhabitants and four are European.

The military officials in charge of United Nations operations also come from those same countries. Six countries (Sweden, Canada, India, Finland, Norway and Ireland) have provided more than half of the 118 military officials who have directed PKOs, from their beginning until November 1993. However, the same cannot be said of the 42 special representatives of the Secretary General in some of these operations, who have come from 26 different countries. The list is headed by the United States, with six representatives, followed by Italy, Argentina and Ecuador, with three representatives each.

However, there are also other countries which take part in the PKOs and which do not fit the prototype above. Countries with low per capita incomes, such as India, Ghana, Bangladesh and Nigeria, have collaborated in numerous United Nations operations. Even micro-states, like Fiji, have played a leading role. Spain belongs to a large intermediate group, made up of countries that have taken part in between six and eight operations.

In the coming years we shall probably see more active intervention by military or police forces from Germany (which has already made its appearance in Somalia, Cambodia, Sahara and Georgia) and Japan (which is participating in Mozambique). These countries are candidates for a seat on the Security Council, whose constitution until now did not allow their presence. In June 1992, the Japanese parliament passed a law allowing the sending of civilian and military personnel abroad on United Nations missions, though for the time being without joining combat.

Table 5.8 Countries taking part in most United Nations peace-keeping operations between 1980 and September 1994

	Operations																							Total
	1	2	3	4	5	6	7	8	9	10	11	12	13	14	15	16	17	18	19	20	21	22	23	
Argentina	*				*		*	*		*	*	*	*		*	*	*	*						12
Australia	*			*	*		*		*				*	*	*	*	*	*						11
Austria	*	*			*	*			*		*		*	*	*	*	*	*		*	*	*		15
Bangladesh						*	*		*		*		*		*	*	*	*	*	*	*	*	*	13
Belgium	*			*			*		*		*	*	*		*	*	*	*	*	*	*			13
Canada	*	*		*	*	*	*		*	*	*				*	*	*	*	*	*	*	*		17
Denmark	*			*	*	*	*		*		*				*					*				9
Egypt									*	*	*	*	*							*	*			10
Finland	*	*	*		*	*	*		*		*	*	*	*	*	*	*	*		*				12
France	*	*	*			*			*		*			*	*	*	*	*					*	10
Ghana	*	*	*						*		*										*			11
India	*	*			*	*	*	*		*		*		*	*	*	*	*						12
Ireland	*	*		*	*	*	*	*	*	*	*	*		*	*	*	*	*				*		16
Italy	*	*		*	*		*		*		*	*		*				*						12
Malaysia							*	*	*	*	*				*	*	*	*		*				10
The Netherlands	*	*										*	*		*	*	*		*		*			11
New Zealand	*						*		*		*	*			*			*				*	*	9
Nigeria	*	*	*				*		*		*	*			*		*	*		*	*			12
Norway	*	*	*	*		*	*		*		*	*		*	*		*	*						14
Poland	*	*	*				*		*		*	*	*	*			*	*		*	*			12
Spain									*	*	*	*						*			*			7
Sweden	*		*	*	*	*	*		*		*	*		*	*	*		*		*	*	*		18
USSR/Russian	*						*		*		*			*	*		*	*			*	*		10
Uruguay				*			*				*							*		*		*		10
USA	*				*			*	*		*		*	*	*	*	*	*						9

See opposite page for key.

Table 5.9 Country of origin of the military officials in charge of PKOs

Sweden	15
Canada	11
India	11
Finland	10
Ireland	9
Norway	9
Austria	7
USA	4
Brazil	4
Former Yugoslavia	4
Ghana	4
Australia	3
Italy	3
Others	24
TOTAL	118

One highly illustrative indicator of willingness to collaborate in Peace-keeping Operations can be found in the total military forces each country provides for these operations. In September 1994 there were more than 76,000 military personnel (including troops and observers) from 68 countries working on 16 PKOs. About 40 per cent of this personnel came from just five countries: Pakistan, France, India, United Kingdom and Bangladesh. If we take a longer period, such as from November 1992 to September 1994, we see that 13 countries have provided more than 2,000 personnel, with Pakistan, France and India once again at the head of the list.

Key to Table 5.8:

(1) UNTSO	(6) UNGOMAP	(11) UNIKOM	(16) UNOSOM	(21) UNOMIL
(2) UNDOF	(7) UNIIMOG	(12) UNAVEM II	(17) MINURSO	(22) UNAMIR
(3) UNIFIL	(8) UNAVEM	(13) UNTAC	(18) ONUMOZ	(23) UNMIH
(4) UNMOGIP	(9) UNTAG	(14) ONUSAL	(19) UNOMUR	
(5) UNFICYP	(10) ONUCA	(15) UNPROFOR	(20) UNOMIG	

Countries participating
(number of operations)

18   Sweden
17   Canada
16   Ireland
15   Austria
14   Norway
13   Bangladesh

Source: United Nations, 'The Blue Helmets' (1990), and 'Peace-keeping. Information Notes', No. 1, 1993; 'Summary of contributions to Peace-keeping operations by countries', January–September 1994.

Table 5.10 Countries contributing most military personnel to PKOs (maximum contingents between November 1992 and September 1994)

	maximum military personnel	*maximum operations*
Pakistan	9,957	6
France	9,058	7
India	5,891	6
Bangladesh	4,332	9
United Kingdom	4,082	5
Italy	3,774	7
United States	3,500	6
Jordan	3,452	4
Canada	3,220	11
Malaysia	2,766	8
Netherlands	2,557	6
Egypt	2,177	6
Poland	2,088	8

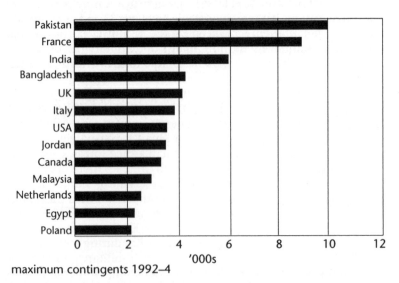

maximum contingents 1992–4

Figure 5.6 PKO military personnel, countries' contribution

During this period, in which three very large operations have taken place (Somalia, Yugoslavia and Cambodia), 78 countries provided the United Nations with some kind of military force, though very unequally distributed. Half of these countries have provided less than 750 personnel, and a fourth, less than 50. Only 32 countries have made more than 1,000 personnel available to the United Nations.

Table 5.11 Maximum military contingents for PKOs (November 1992 – September 1994)

personnel	number of countries
> 5,000	3
3,000 – 5,000	6
2,000 – 3,000	4
1,500 – 2,000	7
1,000 – 1,500	12
750 – 1,000	9
500 – 750	5
250 – 500	5
50 – 250	7
< 50	20

Between November 1992 and September 1994, the number of countries that have made at least 500 military personnel available to the United Nations has remained stable (between 33 and 36 countries) and almost half of them have been European. However, the number of countries that have sent more than 1,000 military personnel has increased considerably, from 14 to 25, due to the African presence. Of the countries that have contributed with more than 3,000 personnel, two thirds are Asian and the remaining third European.

If we compare this contribution of forces to the United Nations with the total volume of military forces for each country, we see that three countries with small populations or small surface areas (Ghana, Botswana and Fiji), all of them with small armed forces, contribute more than 18 per cent of their personnel to United Nations operations, especially those in Mozambique, Somalia, Lebanon, Cambodia and Rwanda. This high proportion bears no comparison with the figures for the second group of collaborators, consisting of nine more significant countries (Ireland, Nepal, Denmark, Norway, Kenya, Finland, Zambia, Bangladesh and Canada), which at some point during 1993 or 1994 contributed between 4 and 6 per cent of their military personnel. A third group of four countries (Uruguay, Jordan, Netherlands and Sweden) have offered between 2.8 and 4 per cent of their forces.

Table 5.12 Countries that have provided personnel for peace-keeping operations

	11/92	3/93	3/94	5/94	9/94
> 500	33	33	36	34	36
Europe	15	16	17	16	17
Asia	9	9	6	7	6
Africa	4	4	8	6	8
North America	1	1	2	2	2
Latin America	2	2	2	2	2
Oceania	2	1	1	1	1
> 1,000	14	17	25	25	25
Europe	8	9	11	12	12
Asia	4	6	6	6	6
Africa	1	1	6	5	5
North America	1	1	1	1	1
Latin America	-	-	1	1	1
Oceania	-	-	-	-	-
> 3,000	3	3	6	6	6
Europe	2	2	2	2	2
Asia	-	-	4	4	4
Africa	-	-	-	-	-
North America	1	1	-	-	-
Latin America	-	-	-	-	-
Oceania	-	-	-	-	-

In the light of these figures, and in view of the continuous obstacles the Secretary General has to overcome in recruiting military personnel prepared to take part in new PKOs, it is worth mentioning once more the marked willingness and adaptability of troops from the Nordic countries, with an average of 3.9 per cent. If every country supplied personnel in the same measure (or in the proportion that Ireland and Canada do), the United Nations would have more than one million soldiers on hand. Whatever the case, the figures show clearly that there are countries in which participation in PKOs is a tradition, a question of state and a vital point in their foreign policy, while in others it is more a possibility depending on circumstances and political opportuneness.

Table 5.13 Peace-keeping forces as a percentage of total armed forces for each country (maximum between November 1992 and September 1994)

	%	troops
Ghana	25.4	1,740
Botswana	19.7	1,202
Fiji	18.8	735
Ireland	6.8	890
Nepal	5.6	1,945
Denmark	5.2	1,468
Norway	4.4	1,870
Kenya	4.3	1,045
Finland	4.3	1,401
Zambia	4.2	903
Bangladesh	4.0	4,332
Canada	4.0	3,220
Uruguay	3.9	974
Jordan	3.4	3,452
Netherlands	3.0	2,557
Sweden	2.8	1,785
World average	0.3	

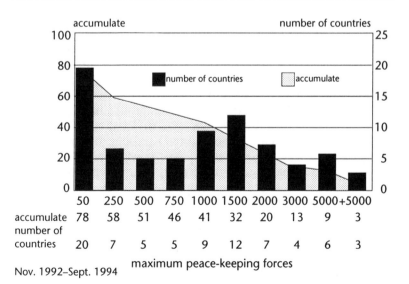

Figure 5.7 Peace-keeping availability, contributions by countries

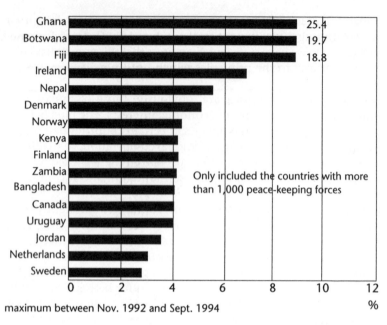

maximum between Nov. 1992 and Sept. 1994

Figure 5.8 The 'blue armies', % peace-keeping/total armed forces

Blue Geopolitics

The sight of blue helmets on television news broadcasts or in the newspapers is now an everyday event, a completely different image to the exoticism or curiosity attached to their occasional appearance in the news just five years ago. This familiarity with 'the blues', especially as a result of their experiences in Bosnia, has nevertheless not been accompanied by reflection as to their real significance and far less on the different reasons that move some countries to take part in United Nations operations. On the contrary, it seems that everyone joins in praising and mythicising their activities to extremes of paroxysm, without realising how essential caution and criticism are in ensuring that something as dynamic and as subject to manipulation as this works properly.

The size these forces have reached is the first thing we ought to look at. At the end of 1994, the military forces (not counting civilian police) available to the United Nations amounted to some 76,000 personnel, an army larger than that of countries like Argentina, Belgium or Sweden and comparable to those of Canada, Hungary or

Holland. This growth has taken place in only three years, from 1990 to 1993. During this period the total number of blue helmets increased sevenfold. Do we have sufficient guarantees that this growth has taken place according to the principles which until now legitimated the blue helmets?

Some of these principles are, obviously, those of impartiality, neutrality and the absence of economic interests. The blue helmets in fact reflected the foreign policies of certain countries that played an especially active part in international co-operation, so that it was only logical that they should also take part in these United Nations operations without expecting any substantial financial compensation in exchange.

However, things today seem to be going very differently. One begins to see a more mercenary attitude as the number of troops and the complexity of the operations increase. We have evidence of this in the figures referring to the 32 countries which have, at some point in recent years, made at least 1,000 personnel available to the United Nations and which have accounted for between 82 and 90 per cent of all United Nations personnel in that time. What these countries have done or not done is therefore very significant.

Thirteen of those 32 countries are rich, five are developing countries or in the process of economic transition and the other 14 are poor. What stands out, however, is that between 1992 and 1994 there has been a clear shift towards an increase in the number of blue helmets from poor countries. In the space of a year and a half, these countries have gone from supplying 43 per cent of the total personnel to 61 per cent. The explanation for this increase lies in the considerable contribution of troops by one group of countries (Pakistan, India, Bangladesh, Jordan, Malaysia and Egypt, especially) during 1993 and 1994.

Next to Pakistan, France is the country that has made most military personnel available to the United Nations during this period, with an average of 7,000 and a maximum of 9,058, considerably more than those immediately following (India, Bangladesh and the United Kingdom). France has sought a clear political benefit from its presence in the PKOs, both through their battalions serving in Cambodia and Somalia, and in its considerable presence in former Yugoslavia, which at times has exceeded 6,000 troops. All together, France has supplied the United Nations with almost 2 per cent of its total military capacity and 4.1 per cent of its professional forces.

But what is the motivation behind the considerable presence of Third World countries, most of them Asian, in such wide-ranging scenarios as Cambodia, Yugoslavia, Somalia or Mozambique? Prestige, money, training, accumulation of merits, geopolitical reasons?

One of the keys to understanding the presence of certain countries in the PKOs is the role they play now in the United Nations system and the role they hope to play in the future. In the same way that France, the United Kingdom and the United States take part, among other things, because they are permanent members of the Security Council, Pakistan is playing its 'blue' card because it is a non-permanent member of the Council. This undoubtedly also has a lot to do with the presence of blue helmets from Morocco, Spain, Argentina, Nigeria and the Czech Republic, countries which have all been non-permanent members in 1993 or 1994.

The considerable Pakistani presence is also due to the fact that Pakistan, alongside India and Bangladesh, aspires to one of the permanent seats (though without right of veto) on the Security Council which could be on offer in the coming years to countries with large populations, along with Japan and Germany, who are certain candidates and, not by chance, recent PKO activists. The involvement of Egypt in these operations, another serious candidate to the Security Council as a leading African and Arab country, could also be interpreted in the same way. A country's involvement in PKOs, and the extent to which it is noticed, has a lot do with its aspirations as regards the Security Council.

Another observable tendency, and a consequence of the interests mentioned earlier, is the progressive Asianisation of the blue helmets to the detriment of the traditional presence of Europeans and NATO members. In March 1993, 53 per cent of blue helmets were European and 51 per cent from NATO countries. Eighteen months later, in September 1994, these proportions had dropped to 40 per cent and 35 per cent, while the proportion of blue helmets from Asian countries went from 23 per cent in March 1993 to 36 per cent in September 1994.

Comparing the figures for November 1992 and September 1994, the number of blue helmets from Canada, Germany, Indonesia and Finland has dropped, and on the other hand there has been a considerable increase in those from Pakistan, India, Bangladesh, Jordan, Malaysia, Egypt, Botswana, Sweden, Zimbabwe and Ukraine. The overall result is a trend towards recruitment of more blue helmets from poor countries.

Only 13 of the 32 countries contributing more than 1,000 blue helmets are industrialised countries with a per capita income of over $12,000. Of the rest, nine have an income of between $1,000 and $3,500 and ten of less than $700. Whereas the 13 richest countries supplied 57 per cent of blue helmets in March 1993, in September 1994 they represented less than 36 per cent. On the other hand, the poorest countries – that is, those with an income of less than $700 per inhabitant – have gone from 28 per cent to 42 per cent. This means that the average per capita income in the countries supplying blue helmets has gone from $12,620 in March 1993 to $7,915 in September 1994. Does this perhaps suggest that we are heading towards a United Nations of poor blue helmets? Does this point to a more mercenary attitude among these forces?

Table 5.14 Continents of origin of blue helmets

	Europe	Asia	Africa	North Amer.	Latin Amer.	Oceania
11/92	24,111	11,221	5,043	3,632	2,090	1,416
	50.7%	23.6%	10.6%	7.6%	4.4%	3.0%
3/93	25,889	11,605	5,011	3,668	2,101	1,227
	52.3%	23.4%	10.1%	7.4%	4.2%	2.5%
3/94	28,482	23,648	10,134	2,974	2,474	817
	41.6%	34.5%	14.8%	4.3%	3.6%	1.2%
5/94	29,386	24,530	8,516	3,260	2,412	799
	42.6%	35.6%	12.4%	4.7%	3.5%	1.1%
9/94	30,098	27,512	10,651	3,605	2,603	1,357
	39.7%	36.3%	14.0%	4.8%	3.4%	1.8%

Blue helmets' wages are, of course, higher than those they receive as soldiers in their own country. But this difference stretches to suspicious degrees when the blue helmet comes from a very low-income country. In this case, a blue helmet can earn in one month what it would take a year to earn when not a blue helmet. The United Nations pays out $1,000 a month in wages for each blue helmet. This is obviously an attractive economic offer for more or less professional soldiers from a handful of poor countries, but it in no way guarantees the competence, professionalism and responsibility of a blue helmet in delicate situations.

If we compare, for example, the number of blue helmets these countries provide with their military expenditure, we can see that the income they obtain through their participation in PKOs can be the equivalent of more than half their national defence budget (in the case of Ghana or Nepal), a quarter (Bangladesh) or much smaller but still significant figures (from 2 to 5 per cent) in Jordan, Pakistan or Malaysia. It is also true that alongside this economic incentive there is the benefit to be gained from taking part in actions which provide very specific training in multinational operations. Furthermore, and this is not always a marginal element, participation in PKOs projects an updated, modern, altruistic image of certain armies which, without this new aura, would be unacceptable because of their putschist or repressive record. In this respect, PKOs help to whitewash and legitimate quite a few armies.

It is also a worrying fact that the blue helmets, to a great extent, come from countries that are not very democratic, if at all. Although it is obviously difficult to come up with reliable indicators of the level of democracy or freedom in the planet's societies, it is obvious that many states do not meet the basic requirements expected if their soldiers, when dressed in blue, are to wield the necessary moral authority and legitimacy. If we look at the 'civil liberties index' established by the Population Crisis Committee, we can see that the average level of the countries that supply blue helmets is low and dropping. Out of a maximum of ten points, the average in March 1993 was of 6.4, and that of September 1994, 5.2, barely managing to scrape through. Furthermore, 40 per cent of countries do not exceed 4 points. That does not mean, of course, that their blue helmets are necessarily evil or despotic, but simply that the governments who send them do not apply at home the system of liberties they expect to impose by force in other countries, through their participation in the PKOs. This illogicality no doubt has its risks.

All of this goes to show that there are a number of different reasons (chiefly geopolitical, financial and image-related) behind the deployment of military units for United Nations operations. The political importance of some operations and the large number of personnel they can mobilise nevertheless calls for a reconsideration of the present system for recruiting blue helmets, which is based more on national interests than on the real demands of the operations they take part in. Getting rid of the national nature of these forces and training them specifically to act as United Nations forces are two of the challenges facing the blue helmets if they are not in future to fall prey to the same contradictions as at present.

The Finances of Peace-Keeping Operations

Payment of quotas for carrying out PKOs involves great difficulties, since the majority of countries habitually delay payment of the contributions assigned to them. In October 1993, for example, Member States owed $1,150 million in this respect. It is also significant that at that time 65 per cent of states had still not paid up their quotas for previous years, a debt that added up to $378 million, of which almost $270 million related to the Russian Federation. One year later, the outstanding contributions to the peace-keeping operations for previous years increased to $526 million.

Table 5.15 Unpaid contributions to the PKOs in previous periods ($ millions)

	10/93	*10/94*
Russia	269.8	316.9
Ukraine	30.7	77.1
South Africa	22.8	33.5
Byelorussia	8.6	20.5
Poland	11.1	11.4
Brazil	0.0	7.2
Iran	3.6	6.2
Libya	2.5	3.8
United States	3.8	3.0
Saudi Arabia	1.5	2.8
Germany	1.5	1.8
Czechoslovakia	8.9	1.8
Others	13.8	53.7
TOTAL	378.6	526.5

The high cost of the last operations prepared or begun by the United Nations has placed the Security Council in an extremely delicate situation, as for the first time ever it finds itself forced to reconsider the traditional financing of these operations. For more than 40 years, United Nations PKOs have cost the Organisation an average of $75 million a year, in no way beyond the means of its budget. Until 1991, no United Nations operation had exceeded a cost of more than $200 million a year. However, the operations in Somalia and former Yugoslavia have each had an annual budget of at least $1,000 million and the one in Cambodia has exceeded $700 million. In 1992, the total cost of these operations was more than the regular budget of the Organisation, which already has more than enough problems trying to get states to pay quotas,[33] and in the middle of 1993 the Secretary General foresaw an expenditure of $3,800 million for all PKOs, a sum exceeding the total cost of the 16 PKOs carried out between 1948 and 1990. It is therefore not surprising that since there is still no generalised conviction that the money spent on peace forces is the best investment to be made in defence[34] and that, in fact, it represents a saving in future military spending, the United Nations Secretary General has considerable difficulty in financing new operations.

Table 5.16 Cost of peace-keeping operations (as at June 1994)

	Location	Troops	Annual cost $ millions
UNPROFOR	former Yugoslavia	36,337	1,900
UNOSOM	Somalia	19,224	1,000
ONUMOZ	Mozambique	5,413	327
UNIFIL	Lebanon	5,219	138
UNAMIR	Rwanda	626	98
UNIKOM	Iraq/Kuwait	1,149	70
UNOMIL	Liberia	368	65
UNFICYP	Cyprus	1,221	47
MINURSO	West Sahara	268	40
UNDOF	Golan Heights	1,061	35
UNTSO	Middle East	219	30
UNAVEM II	Angola	76	25
ONUSAL	El Salvador	222	24
UNMOGIP	India/Pakistan	40	8
UNOMIG	Georgia	22	5
UNMIH	Haiti	(1,267)	1
UNOMUR	Uganda/Rwanda	81	-
TOTAL		71,546 (*)	3,812

Source: United Nations, *United Nations Peace-keeping Operations. Background Note,* July 1994.
(*) Not counting forces authorised for deployment in UNMIH (1,267) and UNAMIR (2,548).

The high cost of some recent operations is obviously related to the considerable numbers of personnel deployed, but also to their scale and complexity and to their civilian or military nature. In the operation in Somalia, for example, expenditure on personnel accounted for 66.2 per cent of the budget between April 1993 and October 1994 (57.4 per cent for military personnel and 8.8 per cent

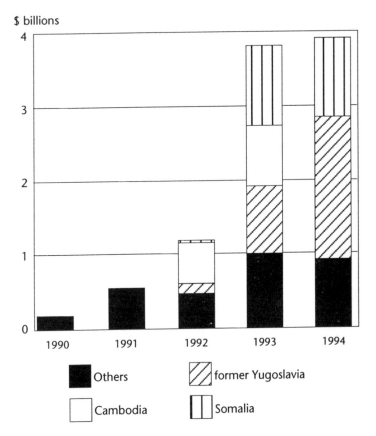

$ billions

Figure 5.9 Peace-keeping forces, annual cost

for civilian personnel), with helicopter rental the second highest expense (10.5 per cent of the budget). In this operation, estimated spending on salaries and food for military personnel for the year October 1993 to October 1994 amounts to $470 million, more than the total budget for 1993 of twelve of the least costly PKOs.

In Cambodia, on the other hand, the operation has had a more civilian character, something which shows up in the budget in the lower military cost (24.1 per cent of the total) compared with the cost of the civilian personnel (26.7 per cent), which includes policing.

In post-conflict phases, futhermore, the United Nations has serious difficulties finding funds to devote to the peace-building stages. When the United Nations itself engaged in peace operations, it did

Table 5.17 Annual cost of some peace-keeping operations (in $ millions)

	UNOSOM Somalia	%	UNTAC Cambodia	%	ONUMOZ Mozamb.	%
Military personnel	607.0	57.4	261.5	31.9	99.9	38.5
Military observers	—	—	32.9	4.0	8.4	3.2
Military detachments	514.3	48.6	197.3	24.1	75.0	28.9
Troops	351.3	33.2	133.6	16.3		
Rations	100.5	9.5	39.0	4.7		
Equipment belonging to detachments	82.6	7.8	21.9	2.7		
Civilian personnel	92.9	8.8	219.1	26.7	45.0	17.3
Civilian police	—	—	107.2	13.1		
International and local personnel	79.0	7.5	102.7	12.5	34.1	13.1
Premises and accommodation	85.4	8.1	71.3	8.7	28.8	11.1
Prefabricated buildings	47.4	4.5	52.1	6.4		
Transport operations	27.7	2.6	59.4	7.2	14.0	5.4
Purchase of vehicles	9.8	0.9	43.1	5.3		
Air operations	111.4	10.5	65.0	7.9	12.6	4.8
Helicopter rental	70.9	6.7	41.5	5.1	9.3	3.6
Aircraft rental	18.4	1.7	5.9	0.7	3.2	1.2
Aircraft fuel	19.1	1.8	13.2	1.6		
Naval operations	—	—	2.9	0.3	—	—
Communications	15.6	1.5	33.6	4.1	9.3	3.6
Other equipment	25.4	2.4	21.2	2.6	3.6	1.4
Supplies (office, uniforms, medicines, etc.)	27.0	2.6	25.7	3.1	3.4	1.3
Services relating to elections	—	—	9.5	1.1	—	—
Mine-clearance programmes	10.4	1.0	3.5	0.4	11.0	4.2
Police-training programmes	18.6	1.7	0.8	0.1	—	—
Air and land freightage	16.9	1.6	28.5	3.5	10.9	4.2
Transport of equipment for detachments	14.7	1.4	14.1	1.7		
Others	20.0	1.9	17.6	2.1	21.2	8.2
TOTAL	1058.3	100.0	819.6	100.0	259.7	100.0

(1) Yearly average for the 18-month period from 1/5/93 to 31/10/94, for which the total budget came to $1,587 million.
(2) Yearly average for the 22-month period from 1/11/91 to 31/8/93, for which the total expenditure came to $1,502 million.
(3) Expenditure for the 12-month period from October 1992 to October 1993.

Sources: UN, documents A/47/916/Add.1, A/47/969.

not think to consult the IMF or the World Bank. In the future, the goal should be to establish a closer link between the United Nations and the Bretton Woods institutions.[35]

Amongst the proposals put forward by the Secretary General himself[36] and by other individuals or organisations for obtaining new funds to guarantee the PKOs are the following:

- The establishment of a Peace-keeping Reserve Fund to cover the initial cost of operations until contributions pro rata are received. In his *Agenda for Peace* Boutros Boutros-Ghali asked for $40 million, a very small amount to pay for operations in the foreseeable future. Soon afterwards, the General Assembly authorised a fund of $150 million (Resolution 47/127). The report by the Ford Foundation[37] asks for a permanent fund of $400 million to be able to begin any operation comfortably.
- The creation of a United Nations Peace Supply Fund, with an initial target of $1,000 million. This fund would be created through a combination of contributions pro rata and voluntary contributions. The voluntary contributions would come from governments, the private sector and private individuals.[38] Once the fund reached the amount foreseen, the returns from the capital invested would be used to finance the initial costs of authorised PKOs. A report by the Palme Commission[39] in 1989 proposed the creation of a fund of $2,000 million for peace-keeping operations. As well as the obligatory contributions, voluntary contributions would be encouraged from states not taking part in the operations directly.
- Loans from the World Bank and the International Monetary Fund.
- Agreement for one-third of the estimated cost of each new PKO to be allocated by the General Assembly as soon as the Security Council decides to undertake the operation.
- establish a tax on arms deals, on the basis of transfers notified to the United Nations arms register.

As regards this last proposal, it is obvious that the positive work carried out by the PKFs must never come to depend on developments in a negative activity such as arms dealing. A tax on arms exports should at most be a provisional and supplementary way of financing either PKOs or other activities of disarmament and verification of arms control.

To understand the scope of a tax of this sort, and since the annual average for global arms exports between 1988 and 1992 came to

$30,200 million, according to the SIPRI, and $50,000 million, according to the ACDA, a tax of 5 per cent on the value of the goods exported would give an annual yield somewhere between a minimum of $1,500 million and a maximum of $2,500 million, so long as it were possible to apply it universally. Since it would be virtually impossible to reach a global commitment as regards payment of this tax (Russia and the United States would have to pay more than $500 million a year, France and the United Kingdom more than $100 and Spain more than $10 million), the most one could hope for would be a tax applied exclusively to the material declared in the register of arms transfers which the United Nations has just created. This volume would be much lower, since notification is not obligatory and the register refers only to a certain type of heavy weaponry.

There is no reason why countries belonging to the United Nations should not ensure contributions of $5,000 million a year for the working of the PKOs. As this sum represents only a small part of global military spending, it would be perfectly reasonable for each country to contribute the equivalent of 1 per cent of its annual military expenditure to the PKFs. In this way the United Nations would receive $8,000 million a year, enough not only to finance the PKOs, but also to pay for other activities of what Boutros Boutros-Ghali calls 'peace-building', as well as a number of disarmament programmes and arms control, verification and conversion programmes, all of them in need of funds.

Other proposals for the financing of the PKOs are that the governments of each continent, or of a particular geographical region, should contribute a percentage of their military expenses to a fund aimed at financing the PKOs in that region,[40] or the establishment of a fixed quota (the same as that already in existence for contributions to the United Nations regular budget), with a pre-established budget ($2,000 million, for example), to which would be added a tax on each country's military spending (variable quota).[41] If this tax were of one part in a thousand, it would provide a further $800 million for the PKOs. The problem is that many countries do not provide very clear military accounting and would not accept the estimates of the United Nations. Even so, it is worth repeating that if PKOs are a collective security expense, all countries should help to finance them out of their traditional military spending. The previous proposal of 1 per cent, though it may seem excessive, is reasonable if one really supports the notion of shared security.

For the time being, however, since no agreement has yet been signed for any State to supply units to the United Nations as foreseen in Article 43 of the Charter, the PKFs depend on the determination and the interest shown by certain states in each case, and operate in a rather improvised fashion. On occasions, this voluntarist mechanism has not been enough to gather the forces needed to undertake a mission, whether to launch it or to keep it going. The temporary and provisional nature of these forces, furthermore, makes for a higher financial cost than if they were permanently available. Training is more complicated because different forces are involved each time and optimum efficiency is never achieved.

The report by the Ford Foundation[42] on United Nations finances includes very reasonable proposals for improving the economy both of the Organisation in general and of the PKOs. It criticises the present method of requesting contributions for each operation individually and says that it would be much more practical to unify the budget of the PKOs, asking states for a single sum to cover all the United Nations foreseen operations, with a reasonable margin for unforeseen expenses. The present system makes it difficult for states to assign budgetary resources, which are only approved once a year, so that the Secretary General can never be sure that he will eventually have access to the amounts requested. The report also suggests assigning regular funds for the training of peace-keeping forces.

The PKFs, therefore, would be cheaper, more operative and more effective if they were stable and permanently on alert, or at least a certain number of them. Although the United Nations Secretary General has not expressed support for the creation of a permanent force, since he feels it would turn out to be impractical and unsuitable[43] and prefers 'a la carte forces' of varying size and composition, his repeated request for states to make available various military units for PKOs, though it makes sense and is necessary for the smooth functioning of the PKFs, is not being attended to with the speed and in the quantities which the circumstances and he himself call for.[44] In his *Agenda for Peace*, Boutros Boutros-Ghali described the concept of 'standby forces', which are not to be confused with peace-enforcement units. In April 1994, 18 countries offered resources totalling some 28,000 personnel[45] which could be called upon in the first instance. The United Nations expects additional commitments from 31 other Member States. This could potentially raise commitments from 28,000 to 70,000.[46] A stable United Nations force, in contrast, as well as solving this aspect, would be the prior step for stimulating the process of reducing national military apparatuses, which could disappear in future if the United Nations manages to become the depository for moral authority and capacity for action, both in pacification and deterrence, as part of a process that would transform current national military capacities into a system of collective security.

A permanent peace force would have many advantages: its mere presence would dissuade certain acts of aggression, it would always be more professional, it would be better prepared to act quickly, it would be able to co-ordinate efforts more efficiently and would considerably reduce expenses. But as Hans Morgenthau pointed out 20 years ago, PKOs will only be efficient and reliable when political interests and the capacity of nations wants them to be. Progress in this direction does not depend on the organisation, or even on the Security Council, but on constant, responsible and solidarity work by all the members of the United Nations.

In short, the PKFs can be organised according to three different approaches which, being successive, could also make up the three phases of a single process:

- The United Nations Secretary General asks some Member States to make military units temporarily available to him for voluntary intervention in a specific operation. This is the current situation.
- The Member States sign an agreement with the Security Council, making previously specified units permanently available. Even if these units were normally engaged in other tasks, they would have to respond to a petition by the Secretary General.
- The Member States sign an agreement with the Security Council to transfer military units to the United Nations for action only in PKOs. This would be the final objective.

In all three phases, a sufficient and reasonable target would be a peace-keeping force made up of 50,000 people, all volunteers and from as large a number of countries as possible. In case any one should find this figure excessive, I would point out that it corresponds to less than 0.2 per cent of the military personnel existing in the world today.

This model could make use of forces depending on United Nations-linked regional security organs such as the OSCE. A force of this sort would have to be available to the Secretary General for intervention in areas outside their own region (see Chapter 7). As regards the possibility of regional organs taking responsibility for PKOs, there are as many advantages to be found as there are disadvantages. Amongst the advantages, they would probably have a better chance of reaching agreement (because there are less countries involved), and they would have more support from the local population and better chances of finding mediators. Amongst the disadvantages, they would have fewer financial resources, they would not have the whole of the United Nations organisational apparatus behind them and they would have less capacity to confront certain regional hegemonies.[47]

Part of this United Nations force could consist of 10,000 civilians specially trained for the non-military tasks usually involved in many PKOs. Furthermore, many young people could have the opportunity to take part in a new International Civil Service, taking the place of military service, which would depend on the United Nations and be carried out in PKOs.

In view of the special nature of missions in PKOs, which are obviously not the same as traditional military missions, their efficacy would be increased as they would be able to train regularly and specifically to carry out their missions.[48] Special training is necessary for PKFs because their approach, methods and tactics differ from those of conventional military doctrine.[49] The aim of the traditional PKFs is not to enter into combat, but to avoid it, keeping their reply to military attacks to a minimum.[50] A permanent PKF would never be just another army, since its personnel would also have to be trained in non-violent ways of solving conflict and be familiar with techniques of mediation and reconciliation.

In this respect, and at this stage, every country providing units to the PKF would have to revise the teaching in their military training colleges so as to publicise the PKOs and make them part of the overall training of any professional soldier. Professional soldiers would have to be familiar with the philosophy and the tactics of PKOs. There would also have to be special courses for these units and special departments would have to be set up within the Defence Ministries, which would be in close contact with the United Nations departments in charge of these operations.[51] At present, United Nations officers' courses are being held which are designed to teach deployment, organisation, structure and make-up of operations of this type, but they are insufficient. The Nordic countries (Sweden, Denmark, Finland and Norway) have most experience of this type of operations and in training for them, since they have joint training centres for people taking part in peace missions.[52]

Having sufficient logistical support permanently available is also an important condition for increasing the efficacy of PKOs, so that as well as the stocks the United Nations usually has in Pisa (Italy), additional stores could also be set up in different continents. States should ensure the necessary materials were not lacking (vehicles, communications equipment, generators, etc.) and that contracts for the purchase of these materials were favourable to the United Nations. As Boutros Boutros-Ghali has pointed out,[53] as well as supplying these United Nations stores, states would have to commit themselves to set aside certain equipment as specified by the Secretary General, either for sale, loan or immediate donation, and make available at no charge to the United Nations the necessary air or sea transport systems.

In recent years, the operation of some PKOs has been limited by the inability to respond to attacks or provocations. Events in former Yugoslavia provide the most obvious example of this. As a police force of interposition only able to act with the consent of both parties, their efficacy becomes questionable – or is simply annulled – when the parties restart hostilities or fail to comply with the agreed cease-fire. To overcome this obstacle it would be useful if the United Nations could send observers to conflict zones without any state being able to prevent it, with the object of weighing up the real possibilities of a successful intervention.

Although the existence of traditional PKFs, acting as an unarmed peace force, is obviously of value in consolidating certain processes of disarmament, demobilisation or cease-fire, the controversy and the doubts arise over the possibility of creating a peace force that can act as a shield, with greater dissuasive power, though not to be confused with a conventional military force, which is always guided by a more offensive strategy. It has, in fact, been suggested in various circles that it would be a good thing also to have a non-offensive force, but one well equipped with anti-tank and air defence systems, especially for deployment along border perimeters,[54] which would be half-way between a traditional PKF and a classic military force of clearly offensive character and capability.

A further suggestion with reference to the provision of greater dissuasive means for the PKFs is that the United Nations should have a naval peace-keeping force, which would provide support for the land peace force as a maritime police force, blockading, clearing mines, escorting neutral shipping in conflictive waters, verifying disarmament agreements, providing surveillance of enemy submarines and helping prevent ecological disasters.[55] The USSR/Russia has long defended the creation of a force of this type which could be based on a small, stable nucleus in the hands of the United Nations, and which might act in emergency situations alongside national units temporarily loaned to the Security Council for specific missions.

Finally, the existence of a permanent peace force would allow the creation of a new status: that of countries protected by the United Nations. In return for contributing to the upkeep of this force, these countries could dispense with their military apparatus and count on the defensive commitment of the United Nations multinational forces in case of need. There are more than 70 states in the world with a surface area of less than 20,000 square kilometres or with less than one million inhabitants, which could be the first candidates for this new approach, constituting an initial step in a more widespread demilitarisation.

Proposals

- In order to carry out the work of prevention, surveillance or interposition, the Peace-keeping Forces (PKFs) must essentially maintain their present characteristics, that is to act with the consent of the parties involved and use exclusively defensive material.
- These limitations to the PKFs need not invalidate other forms of action by the United Nations which all states must accept, such as sending observers.
- For these criteria to be valid, however, the United Nations must also have forces of another sort with greater dissuasive capacity. Until these forces exist, the PKFs must be authorised to respond in legitimate defence in the face of certain aggressions.
- The PKFs must be able to deploy preventively in an area of tension, when one of the parties involved requests it.
- There should be a permanent nucleus of PKFs, made up of some 50,000 troops, all of them voluntary. This would be cheaper, and its actions would be better co-ordinated, quicker and more effective.
- One part of these forces, with some 10,000 members, would be made up of civilian personnel specially trained for the non-military work of the operations.
- Instead of military service, a new International Civil Service could be set up, which would depend on the United Nations and collaborate in PKOs.
- The security organisations co-ordinated with the United Nations, such as the OSCE, ought to foresee participation in the PKFs.
- The PKFs should also have a maritime element to support the peace forces on land.
- Until this permanent force is set up, Member States could sign agreements with the Security Council so as to make available the necessary units.
- The existence of a permanent PKF could lead to the establishment of countries protected by the United Nations, who in exchange for renouncing their own armed forces would receive protection from the PKF.

- The PKFs must have regular specialist training, in keeping with the special nature of their missions.
- States must revise their military education programmes, with the object of making PKOs part of the overall training of any professional soldier.
- All Defence Ministries should set up a department of co-ordination and collaboration with the United Nations organs in charge of PKOs. The United Nations should have permanent access to the logistics necessary for carrying out its PKOs.
- New stores should be set up in different continents for reserves of material necessary for the United Nations PKOs.
- Member States should make available to the United Nations, free of charge, the air and sea transport systems necessary for PKOs.
- The defence and security of peoples must always prevail over the interests of states and governments.
- The United Nations must strengthen its capacity for intervention in the economic and social causes of conflicts.
- United Nations Member States should guarantee a permanent fund of at least $400 million for the initiation of PKOs, and a global budget of up to $5,000 million a year for carrying them out.
- A regular fund should be set up for the training of PKFs, as well as a stable budget for regular expenses (communications, storage, training, etc.).
- The PKO budget should be unified, instead of requesting assignations for each operation.
- States should devote 1 per cent of their military expenses to a PKO fund, which could also be used for United Nations disarmament activities. This proportion would provide some $8,000 million a year.
- Create a tax of 5 per cent on the value of exports and imports of all weapons declared in the United Nations register of arms transfers.
- Create specialist centres in different continents for the training of civilian personnel taking part in PKOs.
- Encourage and co-ordinate the participation of NGOs in those PKOs that are clearly not offensive.
- Prepare peace culture programmes for conflict areas where PKFs are deployed.
- Establish closer links between United Nations peace-keeping operations and the Bretton Woods institutions.

6

The Use of Force by the United Nations

When mechanisms for prevention and regulation prove insufficient or unable to avert a conflict, which then degenerates into open warfare or into a situation in which elementary human rights are severely violated, we have to pose the question of whether the United Nations can provide a military deterrent capable of halting the escalating conflict and re-establishing a prior situation or imposing a new one, without the necessary consent of the parties involved in the conflict.

Some United Nations peace-keeping operations have failed or been severely limited by the normative and material inability of intervention forces to use force at a given moment. In open conflicts, their presence has simply been prohibited, and the United Nations has had no chance to intervene directly by force so as to impose any kind of new order.

Although the traditionally peaceful nature of the Peace-keeping Forces could be maintained in the future with the object of acting in certain scenarios with the consent of the parties involved, inter-vention by force and without the consent of the parties involved could be necessary to put a stop to certain violent situations, once all peaceful means have been exhausted and certain pre-established conditions for this use of force are respected. The United Nations Secretary General himself has recognised the need to carry out enforcement actions in certain circumstances, especially when cease-fire agreements are not respected.

> All too often the sides involved in a conflict sign a cease-fire which they then fail to respect. In these situations, it is necessary for the United Nations to 'do something' ... The role of the peace-keeping forces (perhaps they should be called 'cease-fire-keeping units') is to give the United Nations a chance to rapidly deploy troops to guarantee the cease-fire by deterrent action on one of the parties involved, or both, if they violate the agreement.[1]

The possible use of force by the United Nations can never be the definitive remedy for putting an end to a conflict, which calls for other, evidently non-military means linked to development, social justice and popular participation. This is recognised by the UNDP in its latest report, when it points out that military force is only a short-term answer:

> When conflicts inside a country displace those between countries, the moment has probably come for the United Nations to have its own permanent military force, especially with the object of building peace. But military might is only a short-term answer. The long-term solution is faster economic development, greater social justice and greater popular participation. The new concepts of human security call for development centred on the people, and not soldiers in uniform.[2]

Even so, certain conditions are required for this type of military intervention to be considered legitimate:[3]

- the cause must be a fair one;
- there must be a clearly defined objective;
- all peaceful resources must be exhausted first;
- damage must be kept to a minimum to avoid unnecessary suffering;
- the principle of discrimination must be respected (i.e. the distinction between combatants and non-combatants);
- those taking part must do so disinterestedly (with good intentions);
- the force must be multinational and legitimated by the UN;
- there must be no 'double-edged' policy (intervening the enemy and tolerating the ally);
- the intervention must have a chance of success; and
- the final result must be a positive one.

The United Nations Charter does not forbid or prevent the establishment of a multinational coercive military force. On the contrary, it contains references to the possibility of 'using force' (Article 44) and 'taking such action ... as may be necessary' (Article 42), as well as recommendations that Member States maintain contingencies 'for combined multinational enforcement action' (Article 45).

In his *Agenda for Peace* of July 1992,[4] the United Nations Secretary General recommended the creation of Peace-Enforcement Units, which would be different from the Peace-keeping Forces (PKFs) in their capacity to react to an imminent or real open aggression. These

Table 6.1 Application of Chapter VII of the Charter (1)

	1993	1994
Angola	• embargo on arms and oil	
Haiti	• embargo on arms and oil • suspension of embargo • embargo on arms and oil • monitoring of embargo	• trade, finance and transport embargo • creation of a multilateral force • authorisation of the use of force • end of the embargo
Iraq	• guaranteeing inviolability of borders • respecting inviolability of borders	• withdrawal of Iraqi troops from the border with Kuwait • authorisation of UN flights
Libia	• freezing of financial assets and boycott of airlines	
Rwanda		• arms embargo • protection of refugees • creation of an International Court • protection of UNOSOM II personnel
Somalia	• extension of UNOSOM mandate • authorisation to arrest and try specific individuals	
South Africa		• end of arms embargo
Former Yugoslavia	• freedom of movement of UNPROFOR • flight ban over Bosnia • general embargo against the Federal Republic of Yugoslavia • safety zone in seven cities • creation of an International Court • authorisation for airforce deployment • reinforcing UNPROFOR • relief supplies in safety zones • authorisation of the use of force	• protective measures for three cities • air support in Croatia • cease-fire in one city • economic embargo against Serbo-Bosnians • suspension of the embargo against the Federal Republic of Serbia • authorisation for the use of the air force

(1) Not including resolutions merely extending mandates for United Nations Operations.

forces would therefore go 'beyond pacification', in that they would be deployed without the express agreement of the parties involved.[5] This sort of force tends to have different names according to the person proposing them: Rapid Reply Forces, Imposition Forces, Intervention Forces, Permanent Peace Forces, Rapid Deployment Forces, Multilateral Force, United Nations Peace Force, Emergency Force, etc.

The idea isn't new. In the 1960s, two legal experts, Grenville Clark and Louis Sohn,[6] forerunners of today's internationalism, proposed the creation of a permanent United Nations Peace Force under the control of a United Nations Military Staff Committee formed exclusively of small nations. This force would be equipped with the most advanced conventional weapons and even a small nuclear arsenal and would have two components: a permanent force of 200,000 to 400,000 troops, always available, and a Peace Reserve Force of 300,000 to 600,000 troops. These forces would be distributed all over the world. The United Nations would maintain its own bases and its investigation and logistics infrastructure. As Clark and Sohn see it, however, this new force would only make sense if in return all national arms and armies were eliminated, something they believe could take place in a period of 13 years. Events have proved very different.

In the opinion of Boutros Boutros-Ghali, these units would have the following characteristics:

- they would act in clearly defined circumstances;
- they would act with a previously specified mandate;
- they would come from United Nations Member States;
- they would be permanently on alert;
- they would be made up of volunteers;
- they would be better armed than the Peace-keeping Forces;
- they would receive special training in their respective countries; and
- they could only be deployed and operate with the consent of the Security Council.

Boutros Boutros-Ghali is not asking for forces of his own, at least for the time being. He is requesting semi-permanent forces based on already existing national units, which would be made available to him by Member States. In this way, the Secretary General would have 'a la carte' forces adaptable to different situations.

Before using these imposition forces, the United Nations machinery and diplomacy would first have to exhaust all non-military resources, in particular those included in Article 33 of the Charter regarding pacific settlement of disputes: negotiation, enquiry, mediation, conciliation, arbitration, judicial settlement and the resort to regional agencies or agreements. Whatever the case, the establishment of a dissuasive mechanism of a military nature must be linked to the process of conflict treatment, from the preventive phase up to regulation. This will give greater potential to the preventive action, since the sides involved in the conflict will know for sure that the United Nations is able to put into action its capacity for imposition.

To achieve this deterrent capacity, the United Nations must considerably raise the level of its planning and co-ordination. As Urquhart has pointed out,[7] 'the linking of the different phases of action – from evaluation to pacific settlement to preventive measures to peace-keeping to enforcement – would require a far greater degree of consistency in the work of the Security Council. It would also require serious and continuous staff work and contingency planning, including the availability of forces (Article 43), command structure and logistics.'

A United Nations military intervention force must, as its name indicates, belong to the United Nations, and not to one of the Member States or to a privileged group of them. If it is to wield the legitimacy and moral authority necessary for the use of force, the entire United Nations machinery must take responsibility for the action, both in the decision-making and in the planning and command of the force. All this requires profound changes in the United Nations system, and particularly in the Security Council. As stressed also by Urquhart,[8] it would be absolutely intolerable for an international action of this type to be started only in a situation that threatened the interests of the more powerful nations. Any system of international peace and security must be global and universal, and impartial. In other words, there can be no legitimate use of force unless there is the accompanying reform and democratisation of the United Nations; otherwise the United Nations would once again be taken over by the large powers and the 'double-edged' policy would continue to leave unheard half of the conflicts in existence.

The working of the United Nations during the war in the Gulf, when the organisation became an essential instrument for the geopolitical interests of its most powerful member, is an example of what the United Nations must not do or be. As Falk and Johansen have pointed out,[9] the organisation weakened the collective aspects of security and imposed unnecessary suffering on the Iraqi people, the key commitment of the Charter to consider force as a last resort was prematurely abandoned, the opportunity was lost of making positive use of the United Nations – that is, of fighting Iraqi aggression with the minimum of violence – and the failure of preventive diplomacy and the inability of the United Nations to face situations of crisis were made evident.

To avoid this discriminatory practice which undermines the legitimacy of the United Nations, it would be a good thing if clear and precise patterns of conduct could be established. One possibility would be to open a treaty for signing by all states, rigorously laying out the circumstances in which a collective armed intervention could be carried out for humanitarian ends by a group of countries whose action could be authorised by the majority of the countries signing the treaty. This intervention could take place when large human groups are exposed to violence, when weapons of mass destruction are used against civilian populations or when a state takes no action in the face of natural or human catastrophes in its territory.[10] I agree with Hoffmann when he says that the hypothetical case of a civil war which was likely to have disastrous external effects and cause considerable violations of human rights could be seen by the Security Council as a threat to peace and security between states (Article 39) and it would have to act in consequence without delay, sending United Nations forces with or without the consent of the parties involved.

Article 39 of the Charter
The Security Council shall determine the existence of any threat to the peace, breach of the peace, or act of aggression and shall make recommendations, or decide what measures shall be taken in accordance with Articles 41 and 42, to maintain or restore international peace and security.

Although Boutros Boutros-Ghali himself warns that these units would have to be seen as a way of putting pressure on the parties involved to comply with the provisional measures the Security Council considers advisable, as laid down in Article 40 of the Charter, he is in fact opening the way to the subsequent creation of forces that could act under the powers of Article 43, with very different missions to those carried out traditionally by the Peace-keeping Forces (PKFs).

Article 43 of the Charter
1. All members of the United Nations, in order to contribute to the maintenance of international peace and security, undertake to make available to the Security Council, on its call and in accordance with a special agreement or agreements, armed forces,

assistance, and facilities, including rights of passage, necessary for the purpose of maintaining international peace and security.

2. Such agreement or agreements shall govern the numbers and types of forces, their degree of readiness and general location, and the nature of the facilities and assistance to be provided.

Until very recently, however, the Security Council had not made use of the more coercive measures available to it under Article 42, which legitimates the use of military force by Members of the United Nations to maintain or re-establish peace.

Article 42 of the Charter
Should the Security Council consider that measures provided for in Article 41 would be inadequate or have proved to be inadequate, it may take such action by air, sea, or land forces as may be necessary to maintain or restore international peace and security. Such action may include demonstrations, blockade, and other operations by air, sea, or land forces of Members of the United Nations.

Nevertheless, to comply with Article 42, it would be necessary to put into operation the agreements mentioned in Article 43, which have still not been applied 48 years after their approval in the Charter. In his *Agenda for Peace*, Boutros Boutros-Ghali also requests that the forces made available to the Security Council should be permanently on hand, and not just for certain cases. As the United Nations General Secretary points out, the mere permanent presence of these forces will be enough to dissuade possible peace violations.

Consequently, Boutros Boutros-Ghali's final recommendation on this subject is that the Security Council should initiate negotiations with the Members of the United Nations for the signing of the special agreements described in Article 43, and that in these negotiations the Security Council should be supported by the Military Staff Committee, whose composition could be enlarged to make it more representative, in keeping with paragraph 2 of Article 47 of the Charter, with the inclusion of countries not belonging to the Security Council.

The recommendations of the United Nations Secretary General, therefore, can be summed up in two proposals realisable in the short term:

- Creation of Peace Safeguarding Units, well trained and permanently available to the Security Council, and made up of voluntary forces from the Member States.
- Sign special agreements with Member States for these to make the necessary voluntary forces available to the Security Council.

In the months following the presentation of his agenda, Boutros Boutros-Ghali has repeated and detailed his proposals. In August 1992 he stated that every country ought to be able to form a unit within its own army which by definition could be trained by the United Nations and made available to it within 24 hours. If this were achieved in ten countries, in 24 hours 24,000 soldiers could be made immediately available. Otherwise, he said, it would take the United Nations at least three months to be in a position to send troops.[11]

At the end of October of that same year, the Security Council proposed that Member States offer troops for Peace-keeping Operations (PKOs), with the aim of acting rapidly in international emergencies. At the meeting of the Security Council at the end of January 1992, President Mitterrand guaranteed that France was prepared to make a contingent of 1,000 men available to the Secretary General for Peace-keeping Operations, at any time and within 48 hours. At the same meeting, Russia expressed its willingness to play a practical role in United Nations Peace-keeping Operations and to contribute with logistical support.

Boutros Boutros-Ghali has recently repeated his request that countries provide units that could be available the moment they were needed, and suggested creating a PKO planning unit and an operations centre. Although the request centres on the PKFs, it can also be taken as a call to put into operation the Peace Safeguarding Units. Within months of his request, a small PKO 'situation room' began operating in a wing of the United Nations building. This forerunner of what could become a United Nations Military Staff Room provides the Secretary General with information on everything happening anywhere in the world where the 'blue helmets' are present. This military planning centre is run by a small group made up of one lieutenant colonel and twelve commanders on loan from their respective governments.[12]

For these forces to be really efficient, they should have a good level of command, control, communication and information (C3I). Because of their multinational character, they should also stand out for their high level of co-operation, with which, as Eberle has noted,[13] the United Nations peace forces will function not with C3I but with C4I.

In a speech to the General Assembly on 22 September 1992, the president of the United States, George Bush, encouraged member countries to create special military units which would be available to the United Nations any time a country asked the world for help in resolving a conflict. To President Bush, these units ought to train together and learn from countries like Fiji, Norway, Canada and Finland, which have years of experience in the field of pacification. He also offered North America's bases for carrying out the necessary military instruction.[14]

A variation on these imposition forces is the controversial proposal made by Brian Urquhart in mid-1993 of creating a volunteer military force,[15] a development on an old idea put forward in 1954 by the former United Nations Secretary General, Trygve Lie. Essentially, Urquhart proposes creating a United Nations imposition force which could be deployed before a situation became hopeless, and which would be authorised to take reprisals and could form the basis for a more effective international effort. He suggests that the United Nations should have an international volunteer force ready, initially of some 5,000 men, trained to fight hard and break the circle of violence in the first moments of a conflict, and justifies this use of force on the grounds that in some states, or nascent states, there are often situations of chaos or violence in which traditional PKFs are unable to impose the decisions of the Security Council on irregular militias or other non-governmental groups. These forces would therefore be conceived to fight against irregular forces rather than state military forces, and the chief difference between them and the PKFs would be their voluntary role and their immediate availability.

Comments and criticisms of this proposal were not long in appearing.[16] Some referred to the high cost of the proposal ($1,000 million a year for the 5,000-man force, plus another $15,000 in support) or to the vagueness of the circumstances giving them the right to enter combat. Some comments underlined the need to maintain a suspicion-free balance in the make-up of these forces and strengthen United Nations mechanisms for conflict prevention and solving. The Australian Foreign Affairs minister, furthermore, rightly warned that the Security Council must analyse where and when it can commit itself, to what extent, for how long and with whose money.[17]

The first theoretical and practical steps have therefore been taken towards strengthening the United Nations deterrent mechanism, but for the time being with a reluctance to make full use of the possibilities offered by the Charter itself and, of course, to introduce new variations. Everyone is quite prepared to make one or two units available to the United Nations for peace-keeping operations (PKOs), but objections are raised when it comes to supplying troops for the Peace Safeguarding Units or anything similar, since in all likelihood these would have to join combat. In the 1993 Report on the work of the Organisation, Boutros Boutros-Ghali also pointed this out when he said that:

> It will be evident that the reach of the international community at this time exceeds its grasp. United Nations Forces increasingly find themselves thrust into areas of conflict where major powers are not willing to venture themselves and are reluctant to make the hard choices posed by a new era of challenges to peace.

Resistance is strongest when one raises the question of transferring these units to the United Nations and when certain people say that the process must be accompanied by a progressive demilitarisation of nations. This condition, however difficult and remote it may seem, is nevertheless an unavoidable requirement, since the logical way to make progress in the reinforcement of the United Nations in the field of peace-keeping and imposition is to move naturally towards a transfer of powers to the Organisation. In an initial phase, the PKFs and PSUs could at first be developed under the control of the nations contributing the troops. In a second phase, both types of force would come under United Nations control, as the above pattern illustrates.

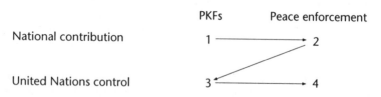

Figure 6.1 National contribution/United Nations control

Unless a real process of disarmament and demilitarisation is begun, the creation both of permanent PKFs and of dissuasive forces under the control of the United Nations will be dangerous and will probably fail. There is no sense in increasing the United Nations' muscle power unless at the same time there is an in-depth revision of current disarmament policy, which so far has not touched on three decisive phases in the arms cycle: research, production and exports.

So long as the world contains an arsenal of weapons the size of the present one – 45,000 fighter planes, 172,000 tanks, 155,000 artillery pieces, more than 1,000 large warships and 700 submarines,[18] as well as millions of rifles, mortars and other artefacts, the planet's insecurity is guaranteed, never mind how many blue helmets are deployed. It is therefore necessary to link the process of disarmament to the strengthening of United Nations peace forces or imposition forces.

If we give a new role to the armed forces through their participation in PKOs, it seems only normal that many arms systems that are no longer needed in these new roles should be reduced or got rid of. The new role of our armed forces has made them obsolete, however much cutting-edge technology they incorporate.

To get from one phase to the next, the Security Council and the United Nations Member States would have to take the following steps:

- Reactivate and make use of the Military Staff Committee, as indicated in Article 47.
- Sign the special agreements indicated in Article 43 making specific forces available to the Security Council.
- Establish the multinational make-up of the force.
- Ensure that it is well trained and permanently available and guarantee proper logistical planning.
- Transfer certain powers relating to military security to the United Nations.
- Reduce national armies until they disappear completely.

As regards the size of a permanent United Nations force, opinions vary widely. This would depend to a large extent on the part they intend to play, on the distinction made between PKFs and Peace Enforcement Forces and on the rate at which the transition takes place. The operations in Somalia and former Yugoslavia have required more than 26,000 personnel to be sent and the one in Cambodia exceeds 22,000, while the war against Iraq called for the mobilisation of hundreds of thousands of soldiers. The United Nations Secretary General has stated that he would need at least 25,000 soldiers for the PKFs, since in mid-1992 the military personnel already involved in PKOs amounted to more than 38,000, which a few months later had increased to more than 76,000. Some analysts have pointed out that the size of the force under the command of the Security Council must be practical and similar to that of an army corps – that is, two or three divisions, with some 35,000 troops, apart from the appropriate air and sea forces.[19] A reasonable estimate would be to ensure a force of 50,000 for PKOs, easy to find if some 30 states sign the relevant agreements and commit themselves, and another 50,000 for the other type of enforcement forces. Since in the first, or current, phase, national armies will still exist, whenever necessary the Security Council could request additional troops from Member States.

One indispensable condition for both forms of United Nations force is that they have an international make-up, with no country contributing more than 15 per cent of the total United Nations effectives or 25 per cent in any given operation, except for those operations requiring a very small number of effectives, in which case the proportions would obviously be higher. Between March 1993 and September 1994, for example, and excluding operations with less than 500 blue helmets, there were 13 cases of countries contributing more than 25 per cent of the effectives in a single operation, and four cases with more than 50 per cent.

Table 6.2 Proportion of one nation's troops in particular PKOs (*) (maximum reached between March 1993 and September 1994)

country	operation	effectives	% total
Bangladesh	UNIKOM	800	69.6
Bangladesh	UNAMIR	915	56.7
Ghana	UNAMIR	352	56.2
United Kingdom	UNFICYP	573	53.2
Austria	UNDOF	461	44.6
Pakistan	UNOSOM	7,057	38.3
Poland	UNDOF	368	35.4
Canada	UNFICYP	521	34.3
Austria	UNFICYP	355	33.0
Finland	UNDOF	355	33.0
Argentina	UNFICYP	391	31.6
Austria	UNFICYP	350	28.3
India	UNOSOM	4,925	27.2

(*) Includes police and military personnel. Does not include operations with less than 500 troops.

Ethnic or religious criteria are unacceptable in the recruitment of United Nations forces, either for peace-keeping or for enforcement. There is no justification for a formula like that put forward in July 1993 by some Muslim countries, with the apparent blessing of Western countries and of the Secretary General himself, of sending blue helmets to Bosnia from basically Muslim countries.[20] Accepting this selectivity in the place of origin of United Nations forces amounts to introducing a sort of 'ethnic criterion' in the make-up of a United Nations force whose mission is in fact to combat 'ethnic cleansing'. If the United Nations forces are to continue to exist, they must be neither Northern nor Southern, Christian nor Muslim, black nor white, but a mixture representative of the reality of international society. Until this is possible, and so long as each country adorns its blue helmets with symbols and distinguishing marks of its own, any United Nations contingent runs the risk of being seen as an intruder.

All the United Nations forces ought to train together in centres set up specially for that purpose and be permanently on alert. The idea of founding some sort of United Nations school of defence is timely and sensible.

To strengthen the decentralisation of the United Nations, make it more operative and economise in the movements of human resources and in logistical movements, these permanent forces should be deployed in various bases, on occasion taking advantage of the many military installations which the large military powers have around the world. Some professionals[21] are of the opinion that the world could be divided into various regions, with a 'forward operative base' (FOB) installed in each region.

Article 47 of the Charter foresees the creation of a Military Staff Committee whose function would be to assist and advise the Security Council on all matters of military security, peace keeping, use of force and disarmament. This measure, traditionally defended by the former USSR, has always been blocked by the negative attitude of the US.

Article 47 of the Charter
1. There shall be established a Military Staff Committee to advise and assist the Security Council on all questions relating to the Security Council's military requirements for the maintenance of international peace and security, the employment and command of forces placed at its disposal, the regulation of armaments, and possible disarmament.
2. The Military Staff Committee shall consist of the Chiefs of Staff of the permanent members of the Security Council or their representatives. Any Member of the United Nations not permanently represented on the Committee shall be invited by the Committee to be associated with it when the efficient discharge of the Committee's responsibilities requires the participation of that Member in its work.

3. The Military Staff Committee shall be responsible under the Security Council for the strategic direction of any armed forces placed at the disposal of the Security Council. Questions relating to the command of such forces shall be worked out subsequently.
4. The Military Staff Committee, with the authorisation of the Security Council and after consultation with appropriate regional agencies, may establish regional sub-committees.

Although it will obviously be needed if a permanent United Nations force is created, and even for co-ordinating or advising on peace-keeping operations, it does not seem such a good thing that this committee, which will of course be made up of military personnel, should be responsible for disarmament and arms control. One cannot be judge and party at the same time. Disarmament already has its own forums for debate within the United Nations, and it is the job of the General Assembly to approve policy decisions in this field. Quite another thing, of course, is that the Military Staff Committee should be involved in technical questions, such as those arising from the verification of disarmament or non-proliferation, but under the corresponding civilian authority.

As regards the possibility of establishing regional subcommittees, this job could be taken on by the OSCE in Europe, since it has declared itself a regional organ under Chapter VIII of the Charter. It would also be a good thing if the Security Council had monitoring centres for regional problems and had the necessary means for making continuous political and diplomatic consultations at a regional level.[22]

The use of force by the United Nations, therefore, involves developing and applying a whole corpus of international law to transform and cut back the sovereignty of states should it be applied.[23] As Boutros Boutros-Ghali himself has admitted:[24]

there is no doubt that the old doctrine of absolute and exclusive sovereignty has not survived; in fact, it was never so absolute as was conceived in theory. Now, it is of the utmost necessity to revive the issue of sovereignty; not in order to negate its essence, but to acknowledge the fact that it can be looked at differently and can pursue more than one objective.

But this will be difficult to achieve until more serious progress is made towards general disarmament, preventive diplomacy is potentiated and a real reform takes place in the United Nations, in particular of its Security Council, abolishing the right of veto, enlarging it to bring it more into line with the demographic reality of the planet and establishing conditions for membership, such as not having debts outstanding with the organisation, having signed and ratified the chief agreements on disarmament and human rights, accepting the decisions of the International Court of Justice and complying with the relevant resolutions of the Council. Only with guarantees of this type can the United Nations really become an instrument of collective security, laying down clear, pre-established rules as to the circumstances permitting the use of force and guaranteeing its non-selective application.

Co-operative security will only reach the United Nations when states on a global level adopt policies to this end, limiting their arsenals, adopting non-offensive defence, renouncing the use of force as a political instrument, helping one another in case of threat and promoting non-violent democratic processes. Obviously, as Randall Forsberg rightly points out,[25] a system of co-operative security would nurture, support, strengthen, teach and guarantee a change in the ethics of international relations.

Until progress is made in this direction, the use of military force by the United Nations will be lacking in legitimacy and plagued by contradictions. Inhibition over the Yugoslav tragedy and offensive excesses in Somalia, where UNOSOM has become a kind of occupying force, are two sides of the same coin and illustrate the unacceptable risk of allowing the Security Council a free hand in deciding when it must intervene and how, without previously establishing the conditions to guarantee a fair and impartial use of that force.

Proposals

- The creation of enforcement forces must depend on progress in the field of general disarmament and preventive diplomacy, on a prior reform of the United Nations, in particular of its Security Council, with the object of guaranteeing that they are used fairly and impartially, and on the establishment of clear rules as to the circumstances permitting the use of force by this organisation.

Once these prerequisites have been fulfilled, these could be the three phases to follow:

1st Phase

- Create United Nations Peace Enforcement Forces of some 50,000 effectives, taken from Member countries' military units, made permanently available to the Security Council.

- Link these forces to the process of reformation and democratisation of the United Nations system.
- Sign special agreements with Member States to make the necessary military forces available to the Security Council (Article 43).
- Open a treaty for signing by states, rigorously defining the circumstances under which the PSUs could intervene without the consent of the parties involved.
- Limit the maximum participation of any one country to 15 per cent of the total PSU effectives and to 25 per cent of the forces taking part in the operation.
- Reject ethnic or religious criteria for recruitment of the troops taking part in an operation.
- Make available to the Security Council the bases and installations necessary for the smooth running of the PSUs.
- Ensure the joint training of these forces.
- Put into action the United Nations Military Staff Committee and enlarge it with representatives from those countries with most experience in peace-keeping operations (Article 47).
- Set up a Peace Enforcement planning and training centre within the United Nations.
- Grant certain regional organs such as the OSCE the necessary powers and resources for collaborating with the Peace Enforcement Forces.
- Set up monitoring centres for regional problems in the regional organs linked to the United Nations.
- Create a regional subcommittee within the OSCE for operations related to the European continent.

2nd Phase

- Transfer full control of the national units made available to the Peace Enforcement Forces to the United Nations.
- Transfer ownership and control of the bases and installations provided in the first Phase.
- Increase the rate of reduction of national military apparatuses.
- Existing military apparatuses will have a purely defensive nature, not provocative.

3rd Phase

- National armies disappear.

7

Europe and Collective Security

For decades, Europe has been divided and at loggerheads due to the presence of two military alliances. NATO and the Warsaw Pact both based their strategies on the build-up of an impressive destructive capacity, to the extent that they became a factor of instability, risk and insecurity for the whole continent.

The end of the Cold War and the political changes that have taken place in the last few years call for a new approach to security in Europe, avoiding the mistakes of the previous doctrine and providing support for the construction of a European space for co-operation at all levels of human activity.

Security, therefore, must not be a concept linked solely to military activity, but must reflect a diversity of efforts, policies and attitudes, from the economic field to the cultural, social and political fields. It is also a concept and an aim that must be shared by a wide range of societies, nations and states which, through a series of commitments, agree on rules of co-operation for the peaceful settlement of differences and a collective approach to the non-compliance of these agreements. A security policy of this type, which depends as much on one's own actions as on the perceptions of others, can become an essential element for the peaceful development of societies.

When I say Europe, I mean Europe, and not just one part of it. Security in Europe, therefore, and whatever the approach taken, is the business of all the countries and societies that inhabit this space, from the Atlantic to the Urals. Otherwise, we would have to speak of security in the NATO countries, or the EC, or something else, but not of Europe.

A security policy must attempt to resolve the real problems that worry or threaten a collective, but without creating new problems as a result of the methods used. During the 1980s, Europe spent no less than $5,290,000 million ($5.2 billion) on her armies,[1] the equivalent of spending $28,000 per family, without this leading to an increase in security or to a solution to its problems. The conflicts of the 1990s demonstrate this. The squander resulting from an incorrect approach to security could not have been greater.

An essential factor in collective security is that the nature and scale of the methods used should fit the aims pursued. Another is that it must not be left to future generations to solve the problems arising from our actions in the present. Security, like development, must be sustainable, in that it must be valid both for the present and for the future.

Although we need to study the form and the circumstances in which military force, as a last resort, can be used, collective security is based on the prevention and regulation of conflicts. Any effort in this field will be a saving in force.

The Threats to European Security

A few years of post-Cold War have been enough to reveal the nature of the new conflicts that are ravaging Europe and the challenges presented by the construction of a new policy of regional security which will have to face up to ethnic and religious conflicts, irredentist nationalisms, xenophobia, ecological conflicts, instability in transition processes to democracy, authoritarianism, poverty in large areas of the East, continuing rearmament, etc.

Although our understanding of conflictive situations has been enlarged, and although these have a multidirectional and multi-dimensional nature, they must not be confused with military threats. Not all problems pose a threat, and not all threats are of a military nature.

In the majority of these conflictive situations, military apparatuses have little or no possibility of acting, and in fact are often themselves 'the problem' or an obstacle to solving problems. Defining and resolving existing conflicts therefore involves demilitarising security policy and channelling each conflict in the direction of the right solution using the means that suit its specific nature.

As the director of the SIPRI has pointed out in reference to Europe:

> political rather than military factors will play an increasing role in maintaining security. Clearly, the threat of armed aggression has substantially diminished. Whereas the sources of instability are of a political and economic, and not military, character, new means and mechanisms must focus on political, ethnic and economic problems, rather than on military ones.[2]

The political geography of Europe is going through a period of change. In the space of a few years, new states have appeared, others have been radically transformed, nationalist claims have proliferated and various ethnic groups are trying to coalesce in a framework that is anything but straightforward. The conflictivity of these movements, proposals or intentions is inevitable, although it need not necessarily take the form of a military confrontation. Out of 18 in Europe between 1989 and 1993, 15 were in the territories of the former Soviet Union and former Yugoslavia. Europe as a region was in stark contrast to others, with a uniform increase in the number of armed conflicts, totalling ten active conflicts in 1993 (six in 1991 and two in 1989).[3] Recognising the existence of these conflicts, attempting to minimise violence in their resolution and finding the right pan-European institutional frameworks in which to discuss them are some of the guidelines for handling them positively.[4]

The case of the former Yugoslavia provides the model of a type of conflict which could easily repeat itself in Europe – although we can also find it in other parts of the world – in which there is a clash of interests and rights: territorial integrity, the right to self-determination, the rights of minorities and the right to self-defence.[5] This conflict has also shown up the extreme fragility of European diplomacy, which has proved incapable of preventing, regulating and solving a conflict within its own borders, so that its possible resolution has been diverted to other organs. As Mendiluce points out,[6]

differences, limitations, contradictions and rivalries lead Europe to hand the problem over partly to the Security Council and the United Nations, which in fact means involving the United States and, to a lesser extent, Russia (Security Council), and getting away from the problems (the failures) using the United Nations as a shield.

All this surrounded by excessive rhetoric and not enough political determination to act.

Declarations on the rights of minorities have always been present in the documents of the Conference on Security and Cooperation in Europe (CSCE) – since late 1994 called the Organisation on Security and Cooperation in Europe (OSCE) – providing the basis for a commitment by this organisation to the resolution of conflicts related to ethnic disputes and the claims of minorities.[7] This is undoubtedly one of the most important challenges for the future of Europe, since the decline in the centralised power of states is stirring up age-old ethnic feelings and nationalist aspirations, as well as reviving demands for solutions to the problems left over from the age of the empires, among them many border disputes.[8] Whatever the case, in view of the vulnerability of many minorities and the instability of some multi-ethnic states, it is not surprising that separatist attitudes and irredentist feelings should abound.

In general, and in view of their internal nature, neither ethnic nor nationalist conflicts directly threaten other states, at least militarily. It therefore makes no sense to plan European military defence on the basis of these conflicts, which must basically be solved by means of non-military security mechanisms and the development of a peaceful multiculturalism which respects the right to be different. Amongst other things, this means that the state must not identify with a type of symbol that represents only one part of the population, and calls for true equality of access to education and jobs, the possibility of obtaining national identity independently of the cultural forms of individuals, state policies that take these cultural differences into account, and maximum decentralisation of political power.[9]

As Rotfeld also has said, referring especially to the countries of Eastern Europe, the extreme difficulty or 'failures in transition processes towards democratic political models, and the questioning of political reforms and attempts to gain popular support by looking for enemies inside or outside the country'[10] constitute a serious threat to global European security and demonstrate the tight correlation between political development and economic development. Continental security calls for both political co-operation to avoid aggressive authoritarianism and real economic co-operation to avoid equally violent frustrations. If Europe wants to share its security, it must also share its financial well-being – in other words, guarantee that the basic needs of its peoples are satisfied. For that reason, and to avoid the formation of a 'third world' in part of Europe, we must weave a fabric of economic interdependence between the west and the east of our continent, without forgetting the needs and the demands of the Third World.[11]

The range of conflicts that are arising in Europe suggests that we are going through a phase of uncontrolled breakdown in security,[12] in which traditional military methods prove to be incapable of resolving conflicts. The moment has therefore come to potentiate confidence measures, policies of prevention, disarmament and human rights across the continent – that is, to develop non-military aspects of security.

In the long term, however, no measure will be effective if it is not accompanied by a global policy directed at resolving underlying problems at the root of conflicts. It is a mistake to think that a solemn declaration of common values is enough to eliminate the source of conflicts.[13] Hence the importance of commitments and of mechanisms guaranteeing the rights of minorities, the free expression of peoples, the respect for free will, shared economic development, democratic training, peaceful negotiation of differences, gradual demilitarisation and other aspects of security.

Documents of the CSCE: a Treasury of Goodwill

In signing the CSCE's most solemn documents – the 'Charter of Paris for a new Europe', in November 1990, and 'The Challenge of Change' (or Helsinki Document), in July 1992 – every single European state accepted a set of common principles, rules of conduct and general commitments in all aspects of collective security in Europe, and very especially in its preventive aspects. But the conflicts that have appeared on the European stage, and those that are foreseeable in the mid-term, oblige us to reconsider the validity of these commitments if they are not accompanied by specific steps to put them into practice, and question the real intention of states and peoples to assume these commitments seriously and coherently. Let me remind you of a few of the introductory paragraphs to the Charter of Paris and the Helsinki Document:

> We affirm that the ethnic, cultural, linguistic and religious identity of national minorities will be protected and that persons belonging to national minorities have the right freely to express, preserve and develop that identity without any discrimination and the full equality before the law. (CP p. 3)[14]

> Respect for human rights and fundamental freedoms, including the rights of persons belonging to national minorities, democracy, the rule of law, economic liberty, social justice and environmental responsibility are our common aims. (HD–6)

> We reject racial, ethnic and religious discrimination in any form. Freedom and tolerance must be taught and practised. (HD–12)

> In accordance with our obligations under the Charter of the United Nations and commitments under the Helsinki Final Act, we renew our pledge to refrain from the threat or use of force against the territorial integrity or political independence of any state, or from acting in any other manner inconsistent with the principles or purposes of those documents.(CP p. 4)

We reaffirm our commitment to settle disputes by peaceful means. We decide to develop mechanisms for the prevention and resolution of conflicts among the participating States. (CP p. 4)

We have put in place a comprehensive programme of coordinated action which will provide additional tools for the CSCE to address tensions before violence erupts and to manage crises which may regrettably develop. (HD–13)

We reaffirm the equal rights of peoples and their right to self-determination in conformity with the Charter of the United Nations and with the relevant norms of international law. (CP. p. 5)

We reaffirm our deep conviction that friendly relations among our peoples, as well as peace, justice, stability and democracy, require that the ethnic, cultural, linguistic and religious identity of national minorities be protected and conditions for the promotion of that identity be created. (CP p. 8)

We express our determination to combat all forms of racial and ethnic hatred, antisemitism, xenophobia and discrimination against anyone as well as persecution on religious and ideological grounds. (CP p. 9)

We will not only seek effective ways of preventing, through political means, conflicts which may emerge, but also define, in conformity with international law, appropriate mechanisms for the peaceful resolution of any disputes which may arise. (CP p. 11)

We have further developed structures to ensure political management of crises and created new instruments of conflict prevention and crisis management ... We have provided for CSCE peacekeeping according to agreed modalities. (HD–20)

It is obvious that intentions are one thing and reality another, very different, thing. Neither the OSCE nor any other European body has the capacity to guarantee or impose these illustriously subscribed resolutions. But this is not all. At state level, the political reforms and cultural processes necessary to put these commitments into practice have not even begun yet. There is no real protection for minorities, because it is still not understood that pluralism, in its cultural, political and social dimensions, is an essential ingredient for European peace and security. The commitment to elaborate mechanisms for the prevention of conflicts is mere rhetoric, since it involves breaking the habit of providing a military response to a situation of conflict. In the last instance, events have shown how untrue it is that 'the necessary steps have been taken for keeping the peace'. This is either false, or else the steps have been taken in the wrong direction.

One paragraph from the chapter in the Helsinki Document on the 'human dimension', referring to national minorities, is a pathetic illustration of how absurd it is, in view of events in former Yugoslavia, to make demands of the following type on signee states:

> They shall refrain from resettling and will condemn all attempts to resettle people by means of threats or the use of force with the object of changing the ethnic composition of parts of their territory.

In view of the xenophobia and the racist brutality to be seen in several European countries, the following passage on tolerance and non-discrimination is equally paradoxical:

> States will take suitable measures to guarantee protection for everybody in their territory against discrimination for racial, ethnic or religious reasons, and protect everyone, including foreigners, against acts of violence for any of these reasons.

There is also a striking contrast between the tough immigration laws of many European countries and this paragraph referring to immigrant workers:

> Create the conditions to foment equality of opportunities with regard to working conditions, education, social security and health services, housing, access to trade unions, as well as the cultural rights, of immigrant workers living and working legally.

Perhaps the philosophy of the CSCE's documents is too compromising for the governments of the signee states. But it nevertheless correctly reflects what the peoples need and to a large extent what some of them are already demanding. It is also worth remembering that Point 8 of the Helsinki Document states that 'the commitments undertaken in the field of the human dimension of the CSCE are matters of direct and legitimate concern to all participating states and do not belong exclusively to the internal affairs of the state concerned'. This paragraph is similar to that approved at the Moscow Conference on the Human Dimension in October 1991. Collective security involves responsible sharing of problems and solutions, one's own and those of others; otherwise, it is best not to start playing around with commitments. No one is obliged to sign the OSCE's documents, but anyone signing must be prepared to accept the loss of part of their sovereignty. This is the price they have to pay to share in the benefits of the security agreement.

Transferring sovereignty to the OSCE means accepting that in certain situations, which should be laid out as clearly as possible, member countries of the Conference agree to intervene in certain internal affairs of other states and, of course, accept that they will be the object of intervention should they be involved in any conflict. Without forgetting how complex and delicate the subject is, this change from the sacred traditional interpretation of sovereignty is what will eventually decide the future of the OSCE: a club for endless debating and negotiating ('the conscience of Europe', as ex-Secretary of State James Baker called it in December 1989), or the organ responsible for security and co-operation in Europe.

The failure to apply and develop the 'European contract' laid out in the documents of the CSCE is therefore a problem of political intention. The framework exists. All it needs is to be truly believed and, subsequently, to be translated into specific political measures.

Conflict Prevention in Europe

The basis of any security policy, whether at state, regional or world level, is conflict prevention – that is, rapid and efficient action at the first signs or manifestations of a process of conflict. Acting in the initial stages can mean stopping it. Not acting, on the other hand, is a guarantee of its continuing and possibly of its entering into stages more complex and more difficult to regulate.

During the Cold War, it was traditional to draw a rough difference between North and South on the basis of the way in which conflicts were handled. In the North, various regulating mechanisms have been created and developed which have avoided, reduced, mitigated or resolved a number of disputes. In the South, on the other hand, the lack of mediating organisms, the accumulation of weapons exported by the North, the colonial legacy, corruption, internal fighting and the failure to definitively resolve conflicts in the past have opened up a number of theatres of war, at a very high human and material cost.

These different tendencies now seem to be repeated in Europe, with a more stable West accustomed to settling its differences through shared institutions, and a less stable East lacking in conflict-regulating mechanisms.[15] We therefore need to set up mediating and regulating mechanisms on a continental level. The OSCE is at the present moment the only organisation with a structure capable of carrying out this task.

As Miall has pointed out,[16] to prevent conflicts in these two areas, action must be taken from two perspectives: first, developing a proper internal capacity in societies to channel and resolve disputes as they arise. It is obvious that the best way to do this is to develop a participative democracy and strengthen civil society. The link between economic development and democracy which I referred to earlier and the existence of a dynamic social fabric form part of the approach to conflict prevention. Secondly, developing an international capacity for channelling internal disputes unresolved within the country, as well as disputes between states. This would lead to a strengthening of the regional or global organisations suited to that task.

Miall also points out that in any conflict there are two phases in which it is easier to come up with a solution. One is the first stage – that is, before attitudes become fixed and actions begin to appear hostile. The other is in the last stages of the conflict, when the cost has become very high and the rival parties are tired. What is important, of course, is to be able to intervene in the first stage – the preventive phase – for which the following are required:

- channels for communication between the parties (avoid incommunication);
- opportunities to air problems (avoid frustration);
- the presence of third party mediators (reduce bad feeling and make suggestions);
- goodwill gestures (avoid stubbornness); and
- procedures for settling conflicts (whether old or new).

Are there the means and the disposition in Europe for solving conflicts peacefully? Developments in the OSCE are encouraging, but they seem to fall short of providing an answer to a highly delicate situation which calls for greater commitment by states and more means for doing the job effectively, even if this upstages certain states that act out of a wish for prominence rather than from conviction.

Europe needs to drop the habit of looking abroad for an explanation for conflictive situations, and get used to foreseeing, accepting, analysing and resolving conflicts arising in the continent, some of which can affect more than one country, although the likelihood is that the majority are of an internal nature. Avoiding and handling internal disputes by non-military means is as important as facing up to external threats with military means.[17] Hence the importance of a large arsenal of non-military techniques and resources making it possible to avoid the use of force.

While the traditional policy of military alliances is aimed at implementing strategies of deterrence and restraint through the strengthening of military structures, the policy of conflict prevention tries to act directly on the threats with the object of reducing them. But to diminish threats and reduce the perceptions of them, we need to promote non-military policies, and especially the economic, political and cultural aspects of security.

Both NATO and the WEU have given verbal support to the strengthening of European conflict-preventing mechanisms. In his speech to the CSCE Conference in Helsinki (2 April 1990), the NATO Under-Secretary General for Political Affairs recognised that:

> the CSCE's capacity for conflict prevention and crisis management must be improved and its efficiency increased. Conflict prevention is essential if Europe is to develop in peace and proseprity. The Alliance came out in Rome in favour of strengthening the CSCE institutions, including the Conflict Prevention Centre.[18]

The report by the meeting of ministers of the North Atlantic Council of 17 December 1992 also stated that:

> the CSCE must play an essential role in the development of more co-operative forms of security, in conflict prevention and in crisis management. We therefore support the strengthening of the CSCE structures and are in favour of endowing it with more authority and operative power in conflict prevention.[19]

In spite of the declared good intentions on both sides, the fact is that the OSCE has neither the right means nor an effective decision-making process to carry out the vital task of conflict prevention, reducing threats, keeping dialogue and negotiation open and avoiding regional escalations.

There are not the resources for an effective early warning. Sending a mission for one or two weeks to study developments in a situation that is already out of control is not the way to prevent a conflict. Generally speaking, fact-finding missions should act before this stage is reached and should be invested with the authority, the impartiality and the guarantees to carry out their task with complete freedom of movement.

Although there is an Emergency Mechanism for dealing with conflict situations which can be put into operation if at least 13 states agree, subsequently consensus is required to approve the actions of the Committee of Senior Officials, which makes it extremely easy to block any decision. The case of the former Yugoslavia has shown this.

This Committee of Senior Officials has the power to decide what must be done to handle conflict situations in the first moments, from making a report to sending peace forces. I agree with Miall when he says that it would be better if these Senior Officials delegated the work of mediation to independent organisations not subjected to state interests and with more capacity for impartial action.[20]

As regards the OSCE Dispute Settlement Mechanism, consisting of a panel of conciliators or non-professional 'dispute councillors', it cannot deal with the internal disputes of states nor with international conflicts affecting 'territorial security, national defence, the territory or claims to jurisdiction of other areas', which excludes from its competence most of the conflicts hanging over Europe. What is more, its only interlocutors are states, when in many conflicts (in their gestation and resolution) non-state actors have as much importance as governments themselves, particularly in ethnic conflicts and the claims of minorities.

The OSCE needs to break away from state structures and find special ways in which these non-state actors and NGOs can take an active part in the identification, mediation and resolution of conflicts. As well as experienced diplomats, this Mechanism should also involve professional mediators capable of actively listening to the parties involved, clarifying the subject of the dispute and exploring settlement options with the affected parties.

As if this were not enough, and as Miall also points out, responsibility for this Mechanism falls to the Conflict Prevention Centre (CPC) in Vienna, which has an important mission to carry out (conflict prevention in Europe) with a minute team (one director, two officials and an administrative staff) and a ridiculous budget ($1 million in 1991). Furthermore, its work centres largely on questions of military security, when non-military aspects are just as important in the development of a conflict.

The High Commissioner on National Minorities (HCNM) is another OSCE body with early warning functions. Here we have someone with experience in this field and of recognised prestige, whose mission is to gather every type of information on national minorities except for that coming from people or movements who practise terrorism or preach violence. To carry out this commendable task, the High Commissioner can be accompanied by a maximum of three people

when visiting areas of tension. The structure of the OSCE is an interesting one, as we can see, but it is quite clearly too small. With a staff
of four and an annual budget of $250,000, the HCNM cannot possibly
comply with such a responsibility efficiently.

To avoid escalation in conflicts, the OSCE should improve the
procedures for sending observers, imposing sanctions and embargoes,
creating security areas and protecting humanitarian aid, as well as
planning a military deterrent able to carry out combat operations.
To control escalation, however, it must have trained and operative
peace-keeping forces, if possible its own, fixed forces, so that European
countries that fail to keep peace agreements can be sure that immediate
action will be taken to avoid an escalation of the conflict.[21]

The idea of collective security based on disarmament and demilitarisation does not mean abandoning the right to self-defence, but
tries to reduce to a minimum the need to exercise that right, by
reducing potential threats and developing mechanisms for conflict
prevention. Furthermore, efficient action through mediation and conciliation in the early stages of a conflict is always much cheaper than
military intervention in the acute stages. There is therefore no sense
in the OSCE working on such a small budget ($3 million a year), when
the NATO administrative apparatus has $2,000 million a year available
to it for planning hypothetical military interventions.

Adaptability of NATO and Marginalisation of the OSCE

Various transnational military defence initiatives of different types
are being developed in Europe alongside one another, leading to serious
confusion over the future organisation of the defence of the continent.

Since the approval in Rome of NATO's New Strategic Concept in
November 1991, which describes the changing nature of the economic,
social and political challenges facing the Alliance countries in the
future, NATO has been paying more and more attention to crisis
management and peace-keeping, with less emphasis on large-scale
mobilisation and more on increasing the capacity for crisis
management using more mobile and flexible forces.[22]

On 27 May 1992 the NATO ministers of defence agreed to offer
their forces for participation in peace-keeping operations under the
orders of the CSCE. A few days before, a figure of some 15,000 men
had been mentioned as a contribution to these forces.

That same month, Germany and France signed an agreement for
the creation of the Franco-German Corps, initially consisting of

35,000 effectives from the two countries. Spain and Belgium have also decided to take part in the corps. This 'Euroarmy' or 'Eurocorps' will be under the joint command of NATO and the WEU, hence the reference to the 'two helmets' its members will wear. It could also act as a peace force, either in NATO missions or in humanitarian operations.

France and Germany have already had a joint brigade since 1990, made up of some 4,000 troops. This mixed brigade will be used by the Euroarmy, which will also have a French armoured division and a German force of the same type.

At the meeting in Rome, the NATO Heads of State and Government said that 'the challenges facing us in this new Europe cannot be approached globally through a single institution, but in the framework of interrelated institutions serving to unite the countries of Europe and North America'.[23] In this way it is accepted that NATO is not in a position politically to carry out Peace-keeping Operations (PKOs) on its own initiative, and it is recognised that only the United Nations and the OSCE can give the required legitimacy to these operations, as they are the only institutions representing the collective wishes of the international community (the UN) and the regional community (the OSCE).

The official criterion, therefore, is that the United Nations and the OSCE take the political decision to intervene, leaving operative responsibility for the operation to NATO under one of the following three formulas:[24]

- making its resources available to the United Nations and the OSCE;
- directing or co-ordinating a PKO on their behalf; and
- providing support for individual participation by allies.

A few months later, on 19 June 1992, the Council of Ministers of the WEU approved the creation of an Intervention Force able to intervene outside Europe, though only under the auspices of the United Nations. It was assigned 50,000 men, all of them from units already assigned to NATO, including the Franco-German Eurocorps mentioned above. Each member of the WEU could decide in each case whether it intervened or not, and under what conditions.

At the same meeting, held in Petersberg Castle, near Bonn, the WEU Member States officially stated that they were prepared to make available to the WEU the military resources of the full range of their conventional forces for military missions directed by a WEU authority and that they could be used for: humanitarian missions; peace-keeping missions; and military missions for crisis management, including peace-enforcement missions. All WEU Member States would set aside military units and military staff to be made available to the WEU for possible missions.

On 1 October that same year, a 'planning cell' was set in progress which has been operative since April 1993 and is based in Brussels. It is made up of 35 military and five civilians responsible for drawing up plans for the use of forces under the orders of the WEU, preparing recommendations for the command and direction of operations and establishing an up-to-date inventory of forces available for use. The creation of a 'diplomatic planning cell' is also foreseen; this would be made up of 100 officials from Member States. Its representatives would travel to areas of tension to avoid conflict escalation, a preventive function which in theory is already carried out by the OSCE. The rivalry and competition between these two institutions is obvious.[25]

In December 1992 the North Atlantic Co-operation Council (NACC), made up of the NATO countries and the countries of the former Warsaw Pact, also offered to co-operate in peace-keeping operations, under the auspices of the United Nations. The Council decided to draw up contingency plans for carrying out operations and organise the necessary armies and manoeuvres, but will decide each one of them when the proposal is made and according to the countries prepared to commit themselves.[26]

In June 1993, NACC created an Ad Hoc Group for co-operation in the field of peace-keeping. At a meeting held in Athens, the countries taking part discussed the criteria and the operational principles of peace-keeping operations. The criteria agreed were as follows:[27]

- A clear and precise mandate from the United Nations or the CSCE.
- Consent of the parties in conflict (Chapter VI), except in operations decided by the Security Council according to Chapter VII.
- Transparency in the operation's objectives and means, and an active information policy.
- Impartiality.
- Credibility (a clear political will and the capacity to achieve the established goals, which must be clear and realisable).

The member countries also agreed to pool experiences and establish practical co-operation in aspects of training, teaching and armies, with the object of preparing common rules for training, increase inter-operability and improve operational efficiency.

When the Euroarmy is ready in 1995, it is intended that NATO's Rapid Reaction Force will also be operative.

This military network which part of Europe is building up – because only a very few European countries are taking part – brings the design of a collective security system based on demilitarisation and conflict prevention to a complete standstill, paralyses the development of an effective OSCE in the fields of diplomacy, mediation and conflict resolution and, of course, wipes out any chance of deterrence by the OSCE.

Obviously, there is no reason why the OSCE should become a military organisation, not even a substitute for NATO. It is probably not the most suitable organisation for carrying out military operations, but it could be the institution responsible for establishing security policies in the continent, including the military component to these policies. In this respect, the logical thing would be for national defence policies to be made subordinate to the decisions of this organisation. The OSCE should decide the policies, and NATO, if necessary, administrate their military component in joint operations, but as part of an overall approach in which NATO and the WEU accept the need for an active process of demilitarisation, general disarmament and conflict prevention driven by the OSCE.

Creating a rapid intervention military force with an offensive capacity, as some NATO countries have done, is putting the cart before the horse, as first of all the following aspects need to be cleared up:

- the global security strategy justifying it;
- the desirable size of the military force;
- the nature of that force;
- how to adapt NATO to the new situation;
- the development of conflict-preventing mechanisms that make such a force a 'last resort'; and
- the circumstances in which their use is justified.

Their very existence somehow jeopardises reflection on the development of European military security, whether through the OSCE or another organisation, and conditions the design of a European peace-keeping force. The offensive nature of these units and their possible use in interventionist operations makes them incompatible with a collective security plan, whose military component ought always to be based on defensive defence, minimum dissuasion, preventive diplomacy and confidence-creating measures. What is obvious is that the envisaged capacity of the Rapid Deployment Forces exceeds the strict necessities of defensive defence.

It seems obvious that Europe can benefit from NATO's experience, from its potential and its organisation, and particularly in the present period of transition, but it is not so clear to what degree and at what level of subordination to other organisations. At the moment, NATO has taken on the following four functions:[28]

- As an indispensable foundation for the stability of European security.
- As a transatlantic organ for allied consultation.
- As an organ of defence and deterrence against any threat of aggression.
- As a factor in the preservation of the strategic balance in Europe.

Having understood the dynamic nature of the process of European construction, NATO is now staking everything on adaptability, especially in the verbal or planning sphere, but always defining itself as an 'essential element in the architecture of Euro-Atlantic security'.[29] Although NATO defines the OSCE as 'the key to the building of Europe', it is in fact reluctant to strengthen it, but prefers to control it. We need only look at the OSCE's annual budget of $3 million, which is equivalent to the cost of a single tank. The annual budget for military expenditure by NATO's European members is 50,000 times the budget of the OSCE. For the moment, endorsement of the military concept of security is still overwhelmingly obvious, and will continue to be so long as the United States looks on NATO as the only way to protect its interests. The North-American approach is to praise the OSCE so long as NATO stays ahead and the OSCE is kept under control and at a minimum as regards both personnel and funds, even if that means reinventing NATO, giving it a new role, a new structure and a new vocabulary.[30]

The manoeuvres to enlarge NATO's field of operations through the North Atlantic Co-operation Council (NACC) are not directed at collective security either, as the countries of the East are considered second-class partners and a terrain is invaded which until now corresponded to the OSCE. Many NATO and NACC plans are really no more than confidence-creating measures which have been under discussion for years in the framework of the OSCE.[31]

The European Community, for its part, also wants to direct the process of European security, although it agglutinates only part of the continent. The Treaty on European Union of 7 February 1992 establishes the institutional framework for foreign policy and security, which for the first time recognises the right to formulate a common defence 'policy', which could lead to a common defence. Furthermore, the Council of Europe has defined as areas of common interest the policy of disarmament and trust creation, non-proliferation and the control of arms exports – that is, aspects already included in the OSCE's usual work.

Confusion, overlapping and time-wasting amongst the European institutions could hardly be worse, and to the difficulty of deciding which are state responsibilities and which are community responsibilities must be added the future powers of the continental organisations. If the transfer of powers to the EC is already difficult,[32] one can easily imagine the resistance by some states to accepting the authority of the OSCE. In any case, rivalry between the OSCE, the EC, NATO and the WEU for control of European security is already affecting the ability to react promptly to conflicts occurring in Europe.

Transforming this imposing European military potential into something in keeping with a new approach to security will require previously defining the object in mind. Unless there is this long-term view the transformation will be an illusion and the most that will be achieved will be slight adaptations and changes of image.

Proposals for putting an end to the present confusion and building a single model of European security are manifold. Most of them agree on the need to abandon old orthodoxies, but reach different conclusions when it comes to specifying which organs need to be changed and deciding on powers.

In a study of the architecture of the new Europe, Günter Brauch proposes for about the year 2000 the creation of a European Security Union, by means of a transition process which would gradually dismantle existing military institutions, armed forces and weapons of confrontation, at the same time as building processes of collective security.[33]

This gradual transition process would have to take into account the following aspects:

- in order to dismantle the Cold War infrastructure it will be necessary to reconvert the arms industry;
- all existing institutions should be integrated in the OSCE;
- economic co-operation inside Europe is the best safeguard for preventing war;
- the co-operation of NATO is essential, especially in implementing arms agreements;
- measures that discriminate against Germany must be avoided;
- the armed forces must be reoriented towards non-offensive defence (philosophy of non-attack, structural incapacity for attack, unlinking of rearmament, etc.);
- European security could combine various regional sub-levels (decentralisation);

- priority would be given to gradual controlled reductions in troops and armaments, and to their verification; and
- the Council of Europe and the European Court of Human Rights could provide the institutional framework for the establishment of a common basis for democratic principles and human rights.

Dan Smith[34] proposes an alternative architecture based on provisionality, on avoiding complete dependence on any one institution and on maintaining a minimal structure, capable of taking on real tasks. In his opinion, the OSCE should be strengthened for dealing with nationalist conflicts, providing aid for refugees and helping in the economic recovery of countries or regions which have suffered a conflict. The EC could include some states from the East as well as non-aligned states wanting to join the Community, in a process of frequent and systematic consultation. The object would be to train in political co-operation, without waiting for the economic situation in these countries to allow perceptible progress in economic co-operation. The EC would co-ordinate the security policies of member states, and NATO, which would not feature so prominently as at present, would administrate those countries' armed forces. Finally, the WEU would remain relatively inactive and without the power to take decisions.

In the opinion of the SIPRI director, one way to consolidate this new security model would be to draw up a general treaty on security and co-operation in Europe,[35] based on the following principles:

- openness and transparency of military activities;
- restriction of threatening activities;
- limitation of armed forces; and
- permanent dialogue on security.

For Rotfeld, the idea would be to build up an effective network of institutions, which would of course include the OSCE and NATO, and the first step would be to sign multilateral agreements on disarmament, confidence measures, conflict prevention, emergency mechanisms, arms trade regulation, non-proliferation, etc.

Since the OSCE is already a United Nations regional organ, some researchers are in favour of creating a similar organisation for matters of European security. Moller proposes introducing the doctrine of non-offensive defence in a regional organ to be called the European Collective Security Organisation (ECSO),[36] comprising all the OSCE states. ECSO's maximum authority would be a General Assembly, which would elect a Security Council and a permanent Secretariat.

There would be two chambers, a state chamber with one vote per country, and a people's chamber with greater representation of the most populated states.

The ECSO Security Council would give orders to a European Collective Military Organisation (ECMO), which would have a small shock brigade made up of some 10,000 troops, with armoured transport vehicles, ten corvettes or frigates, ten transport planes, ten reconnaissance planes and 1,000 paratroopers. The ECMO would have a series of state forces specially assigned to it, as well as heavy weaponry, including weapons of an offensive nature. The national forces, on the other hand, would only have defensive weapons. In this model, no European state would have more than one third of the total military forces.

In the opinion of other analysts, NATO could become an agency at the service of the OSCE and the United Nations.[37]

Independently of the viability of these proposals, it is obvious that if the OSCE is to be a regional organ of the United Nations, sooner or later it must take on functions which at present are assigned to the United Nations Security Council, including those of peace-keeping and the use of force, with a twofold objective: to guarantee the security of the European continent, and to collaborate in the decisions of the Security Council in non-European affairs.

In this way the OSCE would be free to resolve issues of European security, which would be its natural field of action, but it would only be able to act outside Europe with an express mandate from the Security Council. Both NATO and the WEU, if they are to persist, would also be subject to this limitation.

A project of collective security on a continental scale, therefore, can only be approached on the basis of a OSCE with supranational powers acting as a regional organ of the United Nations, as laid down in Chapter VIII of the Charter, and strengthened in the fields of conflict prevention and regulation and disarmament. In this model, NATO and the WEU would have a smaller part to play, providing military forces for peace-keeping or imposition operations, should non-military measures fail, and always assuming that the OSCE had no military forces of its own.

If it is to be operative in this field, the OSCE would have to change the present decision-making process, which is based on 'consensus minus two'. With this form of decision-making and so many countries taking part in the OSCE, it becomes almost impossible to reach agreement on intervention in certain conflict situations. If it is difficult in NATO, with 16 countries, in the OSCE it would be even worse. A majority of three-fifths could be enough to speed up decision-making in the OSCE.

The OSCE and the Peace-Keeping Forces

Although in the Charter of Paris of November 1990 there was no mention of the possible powers of the CSCE in questions of peace-keeping, the Helsinki Document of July 1992, undoubtedly influenced by events in the Balkans, devotes many pages to this aspect, as well as looking at the institutional framework for conflict prevention.

The Committee of Senior Officials (CSO) of the OSCE is the organ entrusted with conflict prevention, and is responsible for advance warning (or early warning), political management of crises, fact-finding missions, peaceful settlement of differences and peace-keeping.

According to the Helsinki Document, the 'advance warning' can be put into operation by a state involved in a conflict, or by eleven states not involved, as well as by the High Commission for National Minorities, the Consultative Committee of the Conflict Prevention Centre, or the Human Dimension Mechanism. There are therefore quite enough different ways of putting into operation this initial preventive mechanism. Whether or not they then work properly is another matter.

The reports of the fact-finding missions, for example, need not be made public if the states involved so wish, which leaves one of the great virtues of this type of investigation – that is, public denouncement of the violation of human rights – entirely without effect.

As regards peaceful settlement of differences, the Helsinki Document foresees the creation of a Court of Conciliation and Arbitration and improvements to existing mechanisms. In October 1992, the CSCE set up two new mechanisms for settling disputes:

- 'Direct conciliation', by which the Committee of Senior Officials (CSO) can determine the nature of a conflict without the consent of the parties involved.
- A Court of Conciliation, consisting of a group of private jurists who will take decisions on disputes in the early stages.

This Court has not been accepted by all countries (the United States, the United Kingdom and Spain, amongst others).

As regards peace-keeping, the OSCE has the power to take part in operations on different scales, using civilian and military personnel, whether to inspect cease-fires, watch over troop withdrawals, help to keep law and order, provide humanitarian or medical aid or provide assistance for refugees – in other words, to act exclusively in the traditional missions of the United Nations Peace-Keeping Forces.

It is also stated that the responsibilities of the United Nations will be taken into consideration and that all action will be within the framework of Chapter VIII of the Charter – that is, as a regional organisation – which means that the United Nations Security Council will have to be informed. In spite of this, it is yet to be seen how the OSCE will be linked to the United Nations to make this collaboration a reality.

The Helsinki Document does specify, on the other hand, three important limitations to the peace-keeping activities of the OSCE:

- they shall not entail coercive measures;
- the consent of the parties involved is required; and
- their duration shall be limited.

In other words, any possibility of using force or acting by force is blocked, which means that there is no question of an intervention during the most acute stages of an open conflict. Although more than one OSCE text explicitly indicate that the commitments made in the field of human rights are of concern to 'all' states, and not 'internal affairs', the creation of mechanisms for acting when these agreements are broken is not accepted, which leaves a gap in the range of treatments for a conflict, since on the one hand there is little interest and few means for peaceful preventive action, and on the other, acting by force is prevented at the moment of maximum tension.

When the peace-keeping forces intervene, therefore, it will be with the consent of the parties and without the use of coercion. The CSO will exercise general political control and will direct operations, and the decision to begin an operation will be reached by consensus in the Council. Prior conditions for its action are also laid out:

- the implantation of an effective and lasting cease-fire;
- the existence of an understanding between the parties; and
- the existence of guarantees for the safety of the personnel.

The mandate will be clear and precise, operations will be directed by the president, and the operations in the area will be commanded by a chief of mission appointed by the president.

The Helsinki Document also states that the forces intervening in these peace-keeping operations can belong to NATO, the WEU or the CIS. These organisations would make available to the OSCE the necessary resources for supporting these activities. It nevertheless seems obvious that the different nature of each of these organisations and the constant political changes taking place in the countries of the East do nothing to help overcome the mistrust entrenched since the Cold War.[38]

At the NATO Spring meeting in June 1992, the Alliance announced that it was prepared to comply with the requests of the CSCE to collaborate in peace-keeping operations. That same month, the Foreign Affairs Ministers of the Commonwealth of Independent States (CIS) also agreed to form a multinational force of 'blue helmets'.[39] At the meeting in Brussels, in December 1992, NATO once again expressed its willingness to support peace-keeping operations carried out under a United Nations mandate, but 'case by case and according to our own procedures'.[40] For the time being, then, the OSCE will not have a contingent of its own, contrary to the proposal made in Helsinki by Sweden, and NATO in fact becomes the OSCE's 'fire brigade'.

Reluctance to give the OSCE the power to use force, with or without military forces of its own, stems from the difficulty states have in assuming a process of disarmament and demilitarisation in the continent. In fact, a peace force and deterrent in the hands of the OSCE would only really make sense if at the same time there was a demilitarisation of the states forming part of this group. The conceptual and organic framework of the OSCE is a call to progress in this transformation process, but so far no one seems willing to entirely abandon the old model of military security based on national armies; hence the mixture of institutions and the confusion and incoherence in approaches to security. National interest rather than humanitarian efforts, international stability rather than peace, are still likely to be driving factors behind the decisions which will be made in the future.[41]

Although the dream of a demilitarised Europe is still remote, it is possible and desirable to point out the paths that could lead us in that direction. If the object is to construct a regional security system and, as Point 23 of the Helsinki Document says, 'no CSCE State shall strengthen its security at the expense of the security of other states', then it is obvious that we must start to agree on disarmament measures that will allow a reduction in national military apparatuses, at the same time as we build up and strengthen the regional security mechanism. It is not a question of adding new structures to existing ones, but of gradually replacing the present network, based on army and state, with one which has a non-military, regional basis, with the object of creating an emergency military mechanism dependent on the OSCE and available to the United Nations, and not in the hands of one country alone.

This emergency mechanism would have similar characteristics to those of a Rapid Reaction Force, although with clearly differentiated training, make-up and missions from those of the present offensive intervention forces. If called on to take action, this mechanism would follow the principles of the 'fair war' doctrine:

- it must be based on international law;
- it must have a chance of succeeding;
- it must be aimed at establishing peace;
- it must discriminate so as not to affect innocent people;
- it must be proportional to avoid making the cure worse than the illness; and
- it must use the minimum necessary force.

There are at present more than seven million soldiers in Europe, including those of the republics of the former USSR. With the exception of some small countries, all the states making up the OSCE have their own armies. Transforming this immense, dangerous military potential into something capable of providing the 50 European States belonging to the OSCE with real security and trust, rather than fear and mistrust, certainly presents a complex challenge, but is nonetheless necessary and viable. The proposal for European defence I shall now lay out, however Utopian it may seem, is no more than a model which sets out to be coherent with the commitments already subscribed by the OSCE Member States.

In the long term, the main objective must be to eliminate Europe's national armies. To take their place, Europe would be given a military structure made up of two basic elements.

First, a permanent, highly mobile, well-equipped and well-trained emergency multinational force, provided with offensive weapons and made up of a maximum of 300,000 professionals from different European countries. No one country could supply more than 15 per cent of the total effectives. These troops would be the OSCE's deterrent nucleus, and would be distributed around different points of the continent. They would guarantee the protection and defence of any state subscribing the OSCE agreements and commitments.

Secondly, national peace-keeping forces, in those countries which, aside from their civilian contribution, wanted and were able to maintain units specially trained for intervention in the OSCE or United Nations peace-keeping operations. No one country would be able to have more than 15,000 members in this type of force, which would be equipped exclusively with defensive weapons. If 20 or 30 countries were prepared to offer forces of this nature, Europe could raise some 200,000 or 300,000 'blue helmets', as well as the emergency forces mentioned above, all of them available for intervention in Europe.

The small countries, or those that voluntarily collaborated in European security without a military contribution, would pay a financial quota (security quota) higher than that corresponding to their size, though they would also be obliged to contribute to civilian aspects of security, according to the size of their population.

Models of this type were proposed and discussed in 1989, at the initiative of the Stockholm International Peace Research Institute (SIPRI), by various military professionals from different European countries.[42] The scenario put forward in these proposals involves cutting down military forces in Europe to at most one-tenth of their present size. The financial saving would be staggering (hundreds of thousands of millions of dollars a year), since the cost could never exceed $50,000 million. With demilitarisation, enormous resources would be freed for non-military aspects of security such as preventing conflicts, combating poverty and economic underdevelopment in many regions, guaranteeing the security of nuclear power stations in the countries of the East, fighting pollution and environmental degradation, increasing economic and technological co-operation with the countries of the Third World, etc.

The existence of a European peace-keeping force would therefore depend on the willingness of European States to reduce their military apparatuses, back up continental disarmament and reinforce non-military aspects of security. In this context, an emergency military force would make sense and would be perfectly compatible with a global demilitarisation programme. Meanwhile, and in view of resistance to disarmament and to the transfer of sovereignty to regional and international organisations, the least that can be expected of states is that they leave the way clear for the development of the OSCE, responsibly face up to the commitments signed in the course of this development, and embody them in internal juridical rules. To sum up, the future of the OSCE depends not so much on the creation of new structures and institutions as on political willingness to improve existing institutions and adapt them efficiently to the circumstances of the present moment.[43]

The OSCE and European Disarmament

The OSCE's activity in disarmament is centred in the OSCE Forum for Security Co-operation, an organisation which according to the Helsinki Document is to co-ordinate work in the fields of arms control, disarmament, confidence-building, co-operation in security matters and conflict prevention. The Forum's objectives are to maintain or reduce to a minimum the size of armed forces, unify the obligations of countries in these matters and negotiate new disarmament measures. The results of the Forum's negotiations will materialise in international commitments.

The Forum has a 'programme for immediate action', divided into three broad sections, with a total agenda of 14 points. This short-term programme could be summed up in four objectives:

- *confidence* (through contacts, exchange of information and the establishment of a code of conduct);
- *transparency* (of doctrine, budgets and production, and through verification of disarmament);
- *non-proliferation*; and
- *conversion* of the military industry.

The experience of the last few years, both in the OSCE and in other forums for disarmament, nevertheless argues against an over-optimistic attitude as regards the willingness of the countries of Europe to progress in this field. It is relatively easy to commit oneself to generalisations, outlines and ambiguities, but this does not always lead to the establishment of more specific measures, either on a national or regional level.

If there is to be any point to the Security Forum and if Europe is to make progress in the field of disarmament, the countries taking part should put into operation specific measures that make for real transparency in their military activities, including arms production and exports. The idea would be not only to control military activity but to reduce it. In the final instance, there can be no control without a prior knowledge of what exists. The Forum should also enlarge on confidence-building measures, again with specific measures (restrictions on manoeuvres and logistics, limitations on offensive weapons, troop reductions, creation of regions under an 'open skies' regime, consultations to co-ordinate military doctrines, development of procedures for preventing and channeling conflicts, etc.).[44]

Reducing military effectives to levels well below that agreed voluntarily at the CFE-1A talks is another must for a European policy of collective security. So long as there are seven countries with armies of more than 300,000 effectives, and one of them (Russia) has almost one and a half million soldiers, it will be very difficult to overcome the old Cold War fears.

Until the day comes when it is possible to do away with national armies, confidence in collective security will grow not so much as a result of increased contacts and meetings between the military of different countries as through their co-operation in simultaneously transforming their present offensive apparatuses into others of a defensive and non-provocative nature. This calls for the introduction of very specific measures (abolishment of bridge-carrying vehicles, creation of corridors without offensive weapons, reduction of amphibious arms, 'voluntary mutilation', etc.), with the object of preventing states from carrying out a unilateral attack.

Pooling each country's doctrines is an important first step, but it is even more important to update old mentalities on security and shake off the inertia and the interests of economic sectors that until now have profited from the old military order. Hence the importance of advancing in the conversion of the whole military cycle, from the research stage to production and exports, and not just in the countries of the East. The commitments involve us all.

In a report on the new dimensions of disarmament presented in October 1992,[45] the United Nations Secretary General quite rightly pointed out the close link existing between disarmament and conflict resolution. Arms build-up, militarism, offensive doctrines and the interests of the military industry, far from increasing the security of nations and of the continent, constitute a genuine threat to it. They form part of the problem, because they feed and aggravate many conflictive situations, even if these stem from some other cause. A safe Europe, therefore, can only be a demilitarised Europe, though it need not be an undefended one. Disarmament, conflict prevention, skilful regulation of conflicts and co-operation in all spheres of human activity are the best arms for its defence.

Proposals

- Potentiate the tripod of conflict prevention, disarmament and human development in the new approach to collective security in Europe.
- Concentrate on resolving underlying problems, whether political, ethnic or economic, and not just on military threats.
- Raise OSCE documents to the category of binding treaties.
- Transfer a large part of responsibility in security matters at present in the hands of states to the OSCE.
- Provide the OSCE with the financial, human and technological resources it needs to carry out its mission.
- Accept the right to interference between OSCE member countries.

- Develop early warning and conflict prevention mechanisms, especially the Conflict Prevention Centre in Vienna.
- Encourage participative democracy and an active civil society.
- Allow greater prominence to NGOs, social movements and other non-state organs.
- Act on the causes of tension to reduce threat perception.
- Develop new confidence-creating measures and give greater transparency to security matters.
- Convert the military industry into a socially useful civilian industry.
- Reorganise armed forces for defence rather than provocation.
- Drastically reduce the number of military effectives.
- Prevent the OSCE from acting outside Europe without an express mandate from the United Nations Security Council.
- Change the OSCE decision-making process, at present blocked by 'consensus minus two', and opt for a majority of three-fifths.
- Accept the rulings of the International Court of Justice and the OSCE's Conciliation Court as binding.
- Move towards the elimination of national armies, at the same time as a collective military security structure is created within the OSCE.
- Set up a multinational emergency force within the OSCE, with a maximum of 300,000 effectives.
- Create Peace-keeping Forces dependent on each state, with a maximum of 15,000 effectives per country.
- Establish 'economic security quotas' for those countries not contributing effectives to the two forces mentioned above.
- Destine the economic resources freed from military activity to satisfying the basic needs of European populations, the reconstruction of the countries of the East, co-operation with the Third World and strengthening non-military aspects of security (ecology, prevention, conversion, etc.).

Notes

Chapter 1: The United Nations' Overdue Reform

1. Maurice Bertrand, 'Le nouveau role de l'ONU', *Memento défense-désarmement 1993* (GRIP, 1993), p. 41.
2. Boutros Boutros-Ghali, *An Agenda for Peace*, United Nations, 1992.
3. Boutros Boutros-Ghali, *Report on the Work of the Organisation 1993*, United Nations, New York, September 1993, paras 456–8.
4. Peter Wallensteen and Karin Axell, 'Conflict Resolution and the End on the Cold War, 1989–93', *Journal of Peace Research*, 31, No. 3 1994, pp. 333–49.
5. Stockholm Initiative on Global Security and Governance, *Common Responsibility in the 1990s*, 1991.
6. Erskine Childers, 'Old-Boying', *London Review of Books*, 18, August 1993, p. 3.
7. Johan Galtung, 'Presente y futuro de Naciones Unidas', in *El Magreb y una nueva cultura de paz*, Seminario de Investigación para la Paz, Saragossa, 1993, p. 373.
8. Daniele Archibugi, 'The Reform of the UN and Cosmopolitan Democracy: A Critical Review', *Journal of Peace Research*, No. 3 1993, p. 305.
9. Bernard Ravenel, 'A la recherche d'une autre ONU', *Damoclés*, No. 57, 2nd quarter 1993, p. 13.
10. Brian Urquhart and Erskine Childers, 'Un mundo en necesidad de conducción: Las Naciones Unidas del mañana', *Development Dialogue*, Nos 1–2 1990, p. 13.
11. Johan Galtung, *El Magreb y una nueve cultura de paz*, Seminario de Investigación para la Paz, Saragossa, 1993, p. 374.
12. Erskine B. Childers, 'Gulf Crisis Lessons for the United Nations', *Bulletin of Peace Proposals*, No. 2 1992, pp. 129–38.
13. Amnesty International, *Peace-keeping and Human Rights,* January 1994 (IOR 40/01/94).

14. On the reform of the interior working of the United Nations system, see Erskine Childers and Brian Urquhart, 'Renewing the United Nations System', *Development Dialogue*, No. 1, 1994.
15. Lothar Brock, 'Negotiations, Palavers and Surgical Strikes', in *The United States, Disarmament and Security*, UNIDIR, 1991, p. 30.
16. Stockholm Initiative on Global Security and Governance, Common Responsibility in the 1990s, p. 10.
17. While the Security Council is exercising in respect of any dispute or situation the functions assigned to it in the present Charter, the General Assembly shall not make any recommendation with regard to that dispute or situation unless the Security Council so requests.
18. Johan Galtung, *El Magreb y una nueva cultura de paz*, Seminario de Investigación para la Paz, Saragossa, 1993, p. 380.
19. One of the proposals made by the Second Conference for a More Democratic United Nations (CAMDUN-2) was precisely the creation of a Second People's Assembly in the United Nations as a subsidiary organ to the General Assembly. It also proposes a regular assembly of public organisations, under the auspices of the United Nations. In Galtung's opinion, this Second Assembly could be made up of government organisations, transnational companies and popular organisations. In his opinion, the best thing would be to create a United Nations People's Assembly elected by direct suffrage all over the world. In 1982, Jeffrey Segall formed an International Network for a United Nations Second Assembly (INFUSA), conceived as a consultative organ of the General Assembly.
20. This is another of the proposals made at CAMDUN-2.
21. Enid C.B. Schoettle, 'UN dues: the price of peace', *Bulletin of the Atomic Scientists*, June 1992, pp. 14–16; The Ford Foundation, *Financing an Effective United Nations*, February 1993, p. 3.
22. In September 1992, President Bush announced to the UN General Assembly that the United States was in the process of resolving the UN's financial deficit caused by the delay in its dues. One year later, and in the same forum, President Clinton made the same promise.
23. On 11 May 1993, Russia used its right to veto for the first time since 1984 with the object of blocking a resolution presented by the United Kingdom to distribute the cost of financing the UN peace forces in Cyprus (UNFICYP) amongst all the members of the organisation. Until then, the United Kingdom had borne a large part of the cost of this mission with a contribution of

$50 million a year. Because of its economic crisis, Russia would not agree to contribute a sum of $2 million a year.

24. The percentage due is calculated according to the average GNP over the last ten years. It would be more reasonable to take a quarterly average, which would reflect economic changes in each country more clearly.

25. The Ford Foundation, *Financing an Effective United Nations*, February 1993. The Ford Foundation has proposed that developing countries whose income per capita is higher than the average for their group and who at present only help to pay for peace-keeping operations with the equivalent of one-fifth of their annual quota to the UN should in future pay the full quota without reductions.

26. Some analysts feel that the cost of peace-keeping operations should be included in the UN regular budget, which would have to be substantially increased.

27. The Ford Foundation Report on the UN's finances also supports this transfer of responsibilities.

28. *The New York Review*, 9 April 1992, p. 42.

29. Daniele Archibugi, 'The Reform of the UN and Cosmopolitan Democracy: A Critical Review', *Journal of Peace Research*, No. 3, 1993, p. 314.

Chapter 2: Enlarging the Security Council

1. In response to the request made by the General Assembly in its Resolution 47/62 of 11 December 1992, the Secretary General invited all Member States to present their written observations regarding a possible revision of the way the Security Council is made up, including the question of increasing the number of members in the provisional programme for the 48th period of sessions.

2. *International Peace Research Newsletter*, No. 1, 1992, p. 36.

3. *El País*, 21 January 1993, p. 2 (supplement).

4. Among the countries which in November 1991 had not yet recognised the jurisdiction of the ICJ as binding are the following: Venezuela, Hungary, Cape Verde, Morocco, Brazil, Djibouti, United States, Russia, China, France, Germany, Italy, South Korea, Iran, Taiwan, Czechoslovakia, Indonesia, Vietnam, Argentina, Saudi Arabia, South Africa, Poland and Turkey.

5. *SIPRI Yearbook 1994*, pp. 767–83.

6. Brian Urquhart, 'The United Nations: From Peace-keeping to a Collective System?' *Adelphi Papers*, No. 265, Winter 1991–92.

Chapter 3: Conflict Prevention

1. Surveillance of manoeuvres and abnormal troop movements, weapons deployment, verification of cease-fire and disarmament agreements, arms trade, etc.
2. There are 100 million international migrants in the world today (2 per cent of the global population).
3. Susan Forbes, 'Une terre inhospitalière', *Réfugiés*, No. 89, May 1992, p. 13.
4. Robert Gurr, 'Ethnic Warfare and the Changing Priorities of Global Security', *Mediterranean Quarterly*, 1, No. 1, Winter 1990, p. 84.
5. The Director General of UNESCO, Federico Mayor Zaragoza, has pointed out time and again the need to set up a peace force specializing in ecological disasters. Some countries, such as Austria and Germany, have also shown an interest in the creation of a multinational force of 'green helmets' to prevent or punish the worst attacks on the planet's natural resources. This proposal has received open opposition from some Third World countries rich in biological reserves (*El País*, 4 June 1992).
6. According to the director of the IAEA Nuclear Security Division, in the former USSR there are 57 nuclear reactors which present a danger because of deficient design or construction. In his opinion, 11,400 million dollars are needed to repair them (*El País*, 23 September 1992). This is, indeed, a very high figure, but the cost of 57 Chernobyls would be even higher. As a last resort, eliminating this threat would mean devoting 1.5 per cent of global military expenditure to this preventive end for one year. This would be an excellent investment in security.
7. Marc Schmitz, *Les conflits verts: aperçu général sur la menace de l'an 2000*, GRIP, 1992.
8. Maurice Bertrand, 'Las Naciones Unidas, reducidas al papel de bomberos', *Cuatro Semanas*, August 1993, p. 7.
9. Hugh Miall, 'Los conflictos étnicos', *El País*, 21 Jan. 1993, p. 3 (supplement).
10. Corneliu Vlad, 'Mesures visant à accroître la confiance et la sécurité dans les Balcans', in *European Security in the 1990s*, UNIDIR, 1992.
11. Peter Newhouse, 'Le système d'alerte avait tout prévu', *Réfugiés*, July 1992, p. 15.
12. Jasjit Singh, 'Removing the Scourge of War', in *The United Nations, Disarmament and Security*, UNIDIR, 1991, p. 43.

13. Hans Binnendijk, 'Europe Needs a Framework for the Peace', *International Herald Tribune*, 9 July 1992.
14. Stockholm Initiative on Global Security and Governance, *Common Responsibility in the 1990s*, 1991.
15. As long ago as 1978, France proposed creating an international agency for arms control by satellite. At an initial stage, the idea was turned down by the United States and the USSR. Later, the USSR expressed support for the initiative.
16. Michael G. Renner, 'A Force for Peace', *World Watch*, July–August 1992, p. 31.
17. Robert C. Johansen, 'Lessons for collective security', *World Policy Journal*, Summer 1991.
18. Trevor Findlay, 'Multilateral conflict prevention, management and resolution', *SIPRI Yearbook 1994*, Oxford University Press, 1994, pp. 19–20.
19 United Nations, *1990 Report by the Secretary General on the Organisation's activity*, 1991.
20. United Nations, A/RES/46/59, 10 December 1991.
21. I share the opinion of some analysts that the Secretary General should have the power to send a mission on his own initiative and without authorisation by the Security Council.
22. In 1967, the United Nations General Assembly approved Resolution 2329, which recognised the usefulness of impartial investigations as a means of resolving conflicts. In addition, since 1962 the UN representative for Holland has on several occasions suggested that a mechanism be set up within the Organisation to carry out impartial investigations into conflict situations.
23. More specifically, Robert C. Johansen has suggested that the Secretary General should be authorised to station unarmed United Nations Observers, at any moment, along a 10 km-wide border corridor anywhere in the world, without the need for consent from the rival parties.
24. Palme Commission, 'Final Declaration by the Palme Commission on Disarmament and Security Issues (Stockholm, 14 April 1989)', *Disarmament*, XIII, No. 1, 1990, p. 192.
25. Lothar Brock, 'Negotiations, Palavers and Surgical Strikes', in *The United Nations, Disarmament and Security*, UNIDIR, 1991, p. 31.
26. Boutros Boutros-Ghali, *An Agenda for Peace*, United Nations, July 1992.
27. In his Report for 1992, Boutros Boutros-Ghali pointed out that between January and September 1992, the United Nations had carried out 75 diplomatic missions of fact-finding, representation and good offices.

28. In 1993, the Court dealt with an unprecedented twelve cases and passed judgment on two of them.
29. In 1984, the United States withdrew their declared acceptance of compulsory jurisdiction when the Court ruled against them and condemned the mining of Nicaraguan ports. In 1988, when it came to ratifying the convention on genocide, the United States expressed its reserve over the Court's authority to deal with these cases.
30. The United States has not yet ratified the United Nations convention prohibiting torture, or the Pact defending civil and political rights.
31. Daniele Archibugi, 'Riforma dell'ONU e democrazia cosmopolitica', *Giano*, No. 11, 1992, p. 109.
32. Tad Daley, 'Can the UN stretch to fit its future?', *Bulletin of the Atomic Scientists*, April 1992, p. 39.
33. Olivier Corten and Pierre Klein, 'Le nouvel ordre mondial: un role nouveau pour l'ONU?', *Memento défense-désarmement 1992*, GRIP, 1992, pp. 89–98.
34. Among the loudest of the Security Council's many silences are those over the occupation of Timor by Indonesia, the occupation of Cyprus by Turkey, the attacks by Turkey against the Kurds and violations of human rights in countries like Saudi Arabia, Kuwait or Syria.
35. *United Nations Chronicle*, June 1992, pp. 4–9.
36. Brian Urquhart and Erskine Childers, 'Un mundo en necesidad de conducción: Las Naciones Unidas del mañana', *Development Dialogue*, Nos 1–2, 1990, p. 13.
37. Maurice Bertrand, 'L'ONU a-t-elle un avenir?', *Damoclès*, No. 57, 2nd quarter 1993, p. 38.
38. Brian Urquhart, 'Learning from the Gulf', *The New York Review of Books*, No. 5, 7 March 1991, p. 34.

Chapter 4: Humanitarian Intervention

1. Peter Malanczuk, *Humanitarian Intervention and the Legitimacy of the Use of Force*, Het Spinhuis, Amsterdam, 1993, pp. 1 and 3. (A book with an excellent bibliography on this subject.)
2. Bernard Ravenel, 'A la recherche d'une autre ONU', *Damoclés*, No. 57, 2nd quarter 1993, p. 15.
3. Alain Joxe, 'Humanitarismo e imperios', *Cuatro semanas*, No. 1, February 1993, p. 4.
4. Médecins Sans Frontières, *Populations in Danger*, John Libbely, London, 1993.

5. *El País*, 14 July 1993, p. 5.
6. Alain Joxe, 'Humanitarismo e imperios', Cuatro Semanas, No. 1, February 1993, p. 4.
7. Graham Hancock, *Lords of Poverty*, Mandarin, 1991.
8. African Rights, *Somalia: Operation Restore Hope. A preliminary assessment*, London, December 1992.
9. Monique Chemillier-Gendreau, 'Ingerencia, caridad y derecho internacional', *Cuatro Semanas*, No. 1, February 1993, p. 9; Ghassan Salamé, 'Un droit mal reçu: le Sud floué', *Le Monde des débats*, January 1993.
10. Ghassan Salamé, 'Un droit mal reçu: le Sud floué', *Le Monde des débats*, January 1993.
11. Gérard Prunier, 'Humanitaire: Un droit hypocrite', *Le Monde des Débats*, January 1993.
12. *El País Semanal*, 9 May 1993, p. 20.
13. Médecins Sans Frontières, *Escenarios de crisis*, Acento Editorial, 1993.
14. *SIPRI Yearbook 1992*, p. 311.
15. ACDA, *World Military Expenditure and Arms Transfers 1990*, Washington, 1992.
16. Rony Brauman, *Populations in Danger*, John Libbey, London, 1993, p. 19.
17. Speech made in Geneva, 5 October 1992.
18. The air forces of the African countries have 150 heavy transport aircraft, with a capacity of 3,220 tonnes.
19. *Revista General de Marina*, February 1992, p. 151.
20. T.G. Weiss and K.M. Campbell, 'Military Humanitarianism', *Survival*, Vol. 33, No. 5, September–October 1991, pp. 451–65.
21. Ibid., p. 458.
22. It is worth bearing in mind that many of today's conflicts are a consequence of the way in which decolonisation took place, and that the borders of half of the United Nations Member States were artificially imposed by the colonial powers.

Chapter 5: The Peace-Keeping Forces

1. Marrack Goulding, 'The evolving role of United Nations Peace-keeping Operations', in *The Singapore Symposium*, United Nations, 1991, pp. 20–6.
2. Maurice Bertrand, 'Las Naciones Unidas, reducidas al papel de bomberos', *Cuatro Semanas*, No. 7, August 1993, p. 6.
3. R. M. Jenner, 'UNTAC: International triumph in Cambodia?', *Security Dialogue*, 25, No. 2, June 1994, pp. 145–56.

4. Boutros Boutros-Ghali, *An Agenda for Peace*, United Nations, New York, July 1992, para. 13.
5. P. F. Diehl, 'A Permanent UN Peacekeeping Force: An Evaluation', *Bulletin of the Atomic Scientists*, 20, No. 1, 1989, p. 35.
6. Maurice Bertrand, 'L'ONU a-t-elle un avenir?', *Damoclés*, No. 57, 2nd quarter 1993, p. 36.
7. Maurice Bertrand, 'Las Naciones Unidas, reducidas al papel de bomberos', *Cuatro Semanas*, No. 7, August 1993, p. 6.
8. Boutros Boutros-Ghali, *Report of the Secretary General on the Work of the Organization 1993*, United Nations, New York, September 1993, para. 6.
9. Human Rights Watch, *The Lost Agenda: Human Rights and UN Field Operations*, New York, 1993, p. 1.
10. AOR 41/02/94.
11. *US Foreign Policy in the Post Cold War Era*, Washington, 24 May 1993.
12. *International Herald Tribune*, 6 August 1993, p. 4.
13. *Inside the Pentagon*, 19 August 1993, pp. 3–5.
14. Department of Defense, *The Bottom-Up Review: Forces for a New Era*, Washington, 1 September 1993.
15. Mariano Aguirre, 'Estados Unidos: cómo buscar y ganar dos guerras y media', *Cuatro Semanas*, No. 8, September 1993, pp. 18–20.
16. *The Defense Monitor*, No. 7, 1993, p. 4.
17. *El País*, 28 September 1993, p. 2.
18. Speech on 27 September before the United Nations General Assembly.
19. Speech on 20 September at Columbia University.
20. Speech on 23 September at the National War College and on 20 October before the Senate Foreign Relations Committee.
21. Speech on 21 September 1993 at the Johns Hopkins School of Advanced International Studies.
22. The White House, *A National Security Strategy of Engagement and Enlargement*, July 1944, p. 13.
23. Carlo Pelanda, 'La pax americana', *El País*, 23 September 1993, p. 8 (supplement).
24. Michael Renner, 'Preparing for Peace', in *The State of the World 1993*, World Watch Institute, 1993.
25. Médecins Sans Frontières, *Populations in Danger*, John Libbey, London, 1993.
26. Hans Magnus Enzensberger, *Perspectivas de guerra civil*, Anagrama, Barcelona, 1994.

27. Michael Renner, 'Critical Juncture: The Future of Peacekeeping', *World Watch Paper*, No. 114, May 1993, p. 9.
28. Michael G. Renner, *A Force for Peace*, World Watch, July/August 1992, p. 28.
29. A study by the Ford Foundation indicates possible future scenarios for the Peace-keeping Forces in Sudan, Afghanistan, Liberia, Kosovo, Macedonia, the Middle East, Nagorno-Karabakh, Myanmar, Sri Lanka and Kurdistan, amongst others.
30. Sweden has sent more than 65,000 people on this type of operation. In May 1994 it had 1,412 troops on nine operations.
31. In the course of its history, Canada has contributed 85,000 personnel to 35 different operations. In May 1994 it had 2,406 people working on nine operations.
32. This does not necessarily imply that they have sent the largest number of troops.
33. In January 1993, which is when the majority of states should pay their annual quota, only 18 countries, which cover 18 per cent of the budget, were up to date with payments.
34. I agree with Boutros Boutros-Ghali that the quotas for peace-keeping operations should be paid out of the budgets of the Defence Ministries rather than the Foreign Affairs Ministries.
35. Alvaro de Soto and Graciana del Castillo, 'Obstacles to Peace-building', *Foreign Policy*, No. 94, Spring 94, pp. 69–83.
36. *Report by the Secretary General on the Work of the Organisation 1992*, United Nations, September 1992.
37. The Ford Foundation, *Financing an Effective United Nations*, February 1993.
38. Boutros Boutros-Ghali also proposes exempting from tax donations to the United Nations.
39. Palme Commission, 'Final Declaration on Disarmament and Security Issues', *Disarmament*, XIII, No. 1, 1990.
40. Hans D'Oruille and Dragoljub Najman, 'A New System to Finance the United Nations', *Security Dialogue*, 25, No. 2, June 1994, p. 138.
41. This possibility has been put forward by the Brandt Commission, amongst others.
42. The Ford Foundation, *Financing an Effective United Nations*, February 1993.
43. Boutros Boutros-Ghali, 'Una nueva etapa para las Naciones Unidas', *Política exterior*, No. 31, Winter 1993, p. 40.
44. The Danish Army has begun recruiting for a 4,500-man strong brigade intended to be ready for peace-keeping and other foreign service from 1995. In the same way, three Baltic states (Latvia,

Lithuania and Estonia) are to form a joint Baltic battalion in 1994. The 650-man battalion will be trained primarily to take part in United Nations Peace-keeping Operations. (JDW, 27 November 1993 and 29 February 1994).

45. In the summer of 1994, the following 21 countries had already reached an agreement to provide troops: Argentina, Bulgaria, Canada, Chad, Czech Republic, Denmark, Finland, Guatemala, Netherlands, Norway, Poland, Senegal, Syria, Spain, Sri Lanka, Turkey, Ukraine, the United Kingdom and Uruguay. In October 1994, the Swedish Foreign Minister told the United Nations General Assembly that Sweden was prepared to establish a peace-keeping brigade. In November of that same year, the Danish government offered the United Nations a force made up of 5,000 soldiers to form part of a Standby Force for preventative or emergency deployments.

46. United Nations, *The United Nations Standby Forces System* (briefing), 16 April 1994.

47. Paul F. Diehl, 'Institutional Alternatives to Traditional UN Peace-keeping: An Assessment of Regional and Multinational Options', *Armed Forces and Society*, Winter 1993, pp. 209–30.

48. In September 1993, the United States and Russia reached an initial agreement for joint training of two of their heavy divisions for PKOs. Training could take place in the two countries and in Germany (*El País*, 10 September 1993, p. 4).

49. In his Annual Report for 1993, the United Nations Secretary General pointed out that training manuals were being prepared for troops, military observers and civilian police, with the object of 'creating an international reserve of peace-keeping personnel with similar skills, knowledge, discipline and codes of conduct, so that they can work together effectively when summoned to do so at short notice' (para. 306).

50. Paul F. Diehl, 'A Permanent UN Peacekeeping Force: An Evaluation', *Bulletin of Peace Proposals*, No. 1, 1989, pp. 27–36.

51. Sam Daws, *Memorandum on an Agenda for Peace*, United Nations Association (UK), 12 November 1992.

52. Finland arranges the military observer courses for student officers. Some 20 countries have participated in these courses. Sweden trains staff officers to be appointed to various international peace-keeping staffs. Norway trains officers for logistics, transport and movement control, and Denmark trains military police personnel. Nordic ministers meet twice yearly to set the guidelines for Nordic co-operation in United Nations military affairs (CSCE 1994, No. 2, p. 7). In this way, Australia has set up a Special Defence

Peacekeeping Centre, which is also open to other countries in the region. Other countries training specially for United Nations peace-keeping include Austria, Brazil, Canada, China, Colombia, Ireland, Luxembourg, Nepal, Netherlands, New Zealand, Philippines, Russia, Singapore, South Korea and the UK (NOD & Conversion, No. 29, May 1994, p. 19).

53. Boutros Boutros-Ghali, Report by the Secretary General on the Work of the Organisation 1992, United Nations, September 1992.

54. John Gerard Ruggie, 'No, the World doesn't need a UNs Army', *International Herald Tribune*, 26–27 September 1992.

55. Michael C. Pugh, 'Multinational Maritime Forces: A Breakout from Traditional Peacekeeping?', University of Southampton, Mountbatten Centre for International Studies, *Southampton Papers in International Policy*, No. 1, July 1992; Paul F. Diehl and Chetan Kumar, 'Mutual Benefits from International Intervention: New Roles for United Nations Peace-keeping Forces', *Bulletin of Peace Proposals*, No. 4, 1991, pp. 369–75.

Chapter 6: The Use of Force by the United Nations

1. Boutros Boutros-Ghali, 'Una nueva etapa para las Naciones Unidas', *Política Exterior*, No. 31, Winter 1993, p. 40.

2. UNDP, *Human Development Report 1993*, p. 3.

3. Anne Julie Semb, 'The Normative Foundation of the Principle of Non-Intervention', *PRIO Report*, No. 1, January 1992; Albert Piris, '¿Cuando intervenir por la fuerza? El recurso a la guerra', *Papeles para la Paz*, No. 47–8, 1993, pp. 63–72.

4. Boutros Boutros-Ghali, *An Agenda for Peace*, United Nations, New York, July 1992.

5. Boutros Boutros-Ghali, 'Una nueva etapa para las Naciones Unidas', *Política Exterior*, No. 31, Winter 1993, p. 41.

6. Grenville Clark and Louis Sohn, *World Peace Through World Law*, 1966, Harvard University Press.

7. Brian Urquhart, 'The United Nations: From Peace-keeping to a Collective System?', *Adelphi Papers*, No. 265, Winter 1991–2, p. 24.

8. Brian Urquhart, 'Learning from the Gulf', *The New York Review of Books*, No. 5, 7 March 1991, pp. 34–7.

9. Richard Falk, 'Una oportunidad histórica', *El País*, 21 January 1993, p. 2 (supplement); Robert C. Johansen, 'Lessons for Collective Security', *World Policy Journal*, Summer 1991.

10. Stanley Hoffmann, 'Delusions of World Order', *The New York Review*, 9 April 1992, p. 41.
11. *El País*, 5 August 1992.
12. Soledad Gallego-Díaz, 'Una legión para la ONU', *El País*, 12 July 1993, p. 6.
13. James Eberle, *Military Aspects of 'An Agenda for Peace'*, United Nations Association (UK), 12 November 1992, p. 27.
14. *El País*, 22 September 1992.
15. Brian Urquhart, 'For a UN Volunteer Military Force', *The New York Review*, 10 June 1993, pp. 3–4.
16. Among those who have commented in successive numbers of *The New York Review* in June and July 1993 are Gareth Evans (Australian Foreign Affairs Minister), Stanley Hoffmann (Center for European Studies, Harvard University), Robert Oakley (former United States special envoy in Somalia) and Anthony Parsons (former British ambassador to the United Nations).
17. *The New York Review*, 24 June 1993, p. 58.
18. Michael Renner, 'Critical Juncture: the future of Peacekeeping', *World Watch Paper* No. 114, May 1993, p. 17.
19. David Cox, *The use of force by the Security Council for enforcement and deterrent purposes,* The Canadian Center for Arms Control and Disarmament, 1991, p. 5.
20. According to *El País* (14 July 1993, p. 4) six Islamic countries offered 21,000 blue helmets to defend Bosnia. In an initial phase they were to come from Pakistan (2,500 troops), Malaysia (1,500) and Bangladesh (1,220). In a second phase, they were to come from Iran (10,000), Turkey (4,000), Tunisia (1,000) and Palestine (1,000). Saudi Arabia offered to send money, but not men.
21. Richard Connaughtor, *Military Intervention in the 1990s*, Routledge, 1992, p. 74.
22. Brian Urquhart, 'Learning from the Gulf', *The New York Review of Books*, No. 5, 7 March 1991, pp. 34–7.
23. Monique Chemilier-Gendreau, 'Ingerencia, caridad y derecho internacional', *Cuatro Semanas*, No. 1, February 1993, p. 8.
24. Boutros Boutros-Ghali, 'Una nueva etapa para las Naciones Unidas, *Política Exterior*, No. 31, Winter 1993, p. 45.
25. Randall Forsberg, 'After the Cold War: A Debate on Cooperative Security', *Boston Review*, XVII, No. 6, November–December 1992.

Chapter 7: Europe and Collective Security

1. ACDA *World Military Expenditures and Arms Transfers 1990*, Washington, 1992. Figures in 1989 prices.

2. Adam Daniel Rotfeld, 'European security structures in transition', in *SIPRI Yearbook 1992*, p. 582.
3. Peter Wallensteen and Karin Axell, 'Conflict Resolution and the End of the Cold War, 1989–1993', *Journal of Peace Research*, 31, No. 3, 1994, pp. 333–49.
4. Dan Smith, 'Entre urgencias e imposibilidades: la arquitectura institucional de la seguridad en la nueva Europa', March 1992, p. 18.
5. James Gow and James D. Smith, 'Peace-making, peace-keeping: European Security and the Yugoslav Wars', The Centre for Defence Studies, *London Defence Studies*, No. 11, 1992, p. 2.
6. José M. Mendiluce, 'El caso de Yugoslavia', *El País*, 23 September 1993, p. 7 (supplement).
7. Hugh Miall, 'New Conflicts in Europe: Prevention & Resolution', Oxford Research Group, *Current Research Report* No. 10, July 1992; published partly in Spanish by the CIP: *Anuario CIP 1992–1993*, Icaria, 1993, pp. 86–116.
8. Brian Urquhart and Erskine Childers, 'Un mundo en necesidad de conducción: Las Naciones Unidas del mañana', *Development and Dialogue*, Nos 1–2, 1990, p. 14.
9. Thomas Hylland Eriksen, 'Ethnicity versus Nationalism', *Journal of Peace Research*, No. 3, 1991, p. 276.
10. Adam Daniel Rotfeld, 'European security structures in transition', in *SIPRI Yearbook 1992*, p. 3.
11. Dan Smith, 'Entre urgencias e imposibilidades: la arquitectura institucional de la seguridad en la nueve Europa', March 1992, p. 13.
12. Serge Sur, *European Security in the 1990's: Problems of South-East Europe*, UNIDIR, 1992, pp. 203–13.
13. Victor Yves Ghebali, 'La CSCE à l'ère du post-communisme: une institution en devenir', *Memento GRIP 1992*, pp. 125–31.
14. The references in brackets are to page numbers (Charter of Paris) or paragraph numbers (Helsinki Document).
15. Hugh Miall, 'New Conflicts in Europe: Prevention & Resolution', Oxford Research Group, *Current Research Report*, No. 10, July 1992.
16. Hugh Miall, ibid.
17. Daniel N. Nelson, 'Snatching defeat from the jaws of victory', *Bulletin of the Atomic Scientists,* October 1992, p. 25.
18. *Rapport UEO*, No. 1306, 13 May 1992, p. 53.
19. *NATO Review*, No. 6, December 1992, p. 29.
20. Hugh Miall, 'New Conflicts in Europe: Prevention & Resolution', Oxford Research Group, *Current Research Report*, No. 10, July 1992.

21. Hans Binnendijk, 'Europe needs a Framework for the Peace', *International Herald Tribune*, 9 July 1992.
22. John Kriendler, 'El nuevo papel de la OTAN: Oportunidades y limitaciones en el mantenimiento de la paz', *Revista de la OTAN*, No. 3, June 1993, p. 17.
23. *NATO Review*, No. 6, December 1991, pp. 25–32.
24. John Kriendler *NATO Review*, No. 3, June 1993, p. 18.
25. GRIP, *Memento défense-désarmement 1993*, pp. 205–6.
26. *El País*, 19 December 1992, p. 3.
27. *NATO Review*, No. 4, August 1993, pp. 30–5.
28. Speech by the NATO Under-Secretary General for Political Affairs at the CSCE Follow-up Meeting, Helsinki, 2 April 1990.
29. Ibid.
30. Daniel N. Nelson, 'Snatching defeat from the jaws of victory', *Bulletin of the Atomic Scientists*, October 1992, p. 27.
31. BASIC, 'NATO 2000', *BASIC Report*, No. 2, 1992, p. 13.
32. The reluctance of Community states to transfer power to the EC for the control of the arms trade is significant. They have not wanted to repeal Article 233 of the Treaty of Rome, which allows the exclusion of arms production from the sphere of the Community.
33. Hans Günter Brauch, *German Unity, Defensive Defense and the New European Peace Architecture: 10 Conceptual Hypotheses*, IPRA Conference, Groningen, July 1990.
34. Dan Smith, 'Entre urgencias e imposibilidades: la arquitectura institucional de la seguridad en la nueva Europa', March 1992, pp. 5–6.
35. Adam D. Rotfeld, *SIPRI Yearbook 1992*, pp. 563–82.
36. Bjorn Moller, 'NOD and stability in a Post-Bipolar World', *Arbejdspapirer*, Center for Peace and Conflict Research, No. 10, 1992, pp. 13–14.
37. André Dumoulin, 'Enjeux et perspectives des forces multinationales', *Memento GRIP 1992*, pp. 165–81.
38. Russian diplomats have expressed concern over the support of the United States and the United Nations for future deployments of the Peace Forces on the Russian periphery, especially as only the United States seems to be prepared to send troops, and in spite of an official North-American document which states that the US will only send troops with the consent of all the parties involved in the conflict (*International Herald Tribune*, 6 August 1993).
39. The essential function of these forces will be to intervene as a force of interposition in the armed conflicts ravaging the territory

of the former USSR, so long as the parties involved request it. Responsibility for training these units will fall to the CIS Armed Forces command and they will be made up of voluntary soldiers and officers from different countries in the CIS (*El País*, 17 June 1992).

40.   *NATO Review*, No. 6, December 1992, p. 28.

41.   'NATO, Peacekeeping, and the United Nations', *BASIC Report* 94.1, p. 60.

42.   Gerhard Wachter and Axel Krohm, 'Stability and Arms Control in Europe: The Role of Military Forces within a European Security System', *SIPRI Research Report*, July 1989.

43.   Adam D. Rotfeld, 'The CSCE: towards a security organisation', *SIPRI Yearbook 1993*, Oxford University Press, 1993, p. 189.

44.   Corneliu Vlad, 'Mesures viasant à accroître la confiance et la sécurité dans les Balcans', in *European Security in the 1990s*, UNIDIR, 1992.

45.   Boutros Boutros-Ghali, *New Dimensions of Arms Regulation and Disarmament in the Post-Cold War Era*, United Nations, January 1993.

Index

health, costs of UN project for,
  13fig
Helsinki Document (1992)
  139–40, 141, 154, 155
High Commissioner on
  National Minorities
  (HCNM) 145–6
human rights
  and international courts 10
  in peace-keeping operations
    78–9
  and principle of non-inter-
    vention 48
  recognition of treaties, 25,
    27fig
humanitarian intervention 48
  instead of conflict solution
    53–8
  NGOs and 54–5, 59–60
  problems of 52, 57–9
  proposals for 69
  spending on aid, 4–5, 16fig,
    63
  transport and distribution of
    aid 62, 65–8
  use of military resources 64,
    66–7

IMF (International Monetary
  Fund) 111
immigration
  European attitudes to 141
  see also refugees
imposition forces *see* military
  force
India
  conflict in 33
  Security Council membership
    21, 23
Indonesia
  conflict in 33
  Security Council membership
    21

information
  and communication, for
    humanitarian ends 64
  Office of Research and
    Collection of Information
    (ORCI) 45
  and verification capacity of
    UN 42
  see also fact-finding missions
International Court of Justice
  (ICJ) 10, 24, 47–8
International Organisation for
  Migration (IOM) 67
intervention, by UN in state
  affairs 48, 89
Intervention force, of WEU
  147–8
Iran
  conflict in 33
  Security Council membership
    22
Iraq
  conflict in 33
  peace-keeping operation in,
    33, 68, 121fig, 123–4
Israel, conflict in 33
Italy, Security Council
  membership 20–1

Japan
  contributions to UN by 14
  Security Council membership
    20, 23
Joxe, Alain 53, 56

Latin-America, and Security
  Council membership
    21–2
Lebanon, conflict in 33
Liberia
  conflict in 33
  peace-keeping operation in,
    33, 74–6fig

Index by Judith Lavender